Potty Training in 3 Days

How to Ditch Diapers By the Weekend

Olivia Maxwell

Olivia Maxwell

Potty Training in 3 Days

How to Ditch Diapers By the Weekend

First published by Coral Cubs 2025

Copyright © 2025 by Olivia Maxwell

All rights reserved. No part of this publication may be reproduced, stored or transmitted in any form or by any means, electronic, mechanical, photocopying, recording, scanning, or otherwise without written permission from the publisher. It is illegal to copy this book, post it to a website, or distribute it by any other means without permission.

First edition

This book was professionally typeset on Reedsy
Find out more at reedsy.com

Contents

Acknowledgments

Introduction

I. PART - I - THE POTTY MINDSET

1. Behavioral Psychology

2. Are You Ready?

II. PART II: TAILORED STRATEGIES

3. The Curious Explorer

4. The Power Seeker

5. The Rule Learner

III. PART III: THE 3-DAY FRAMEWORK

6. Day 1 – Goodbye Diapers

7. Day 2 – Learning by Mishap

8. Day 3 – Mastery and Motivation

IV. PART IV: TROUBLESHOOTING

9. Beyond Three Days

10. Personality Perspective

V. PART V: REINFORCEMENT

11. Your Mindset Matters

12. Real Success

13. APPENDIX: Tools, Charts & Resources

Acknowledgments

Thanks to my mom and dad for showing me what real patience is. Only when I was kneeling in the living room, applauding a toddler for using the bathroom at the appropriate time, did I truly understand your quiet strength. Your love gave me the strength to grow and the peace to move on.

I didn't write this book in a peaceful hut or a pristine office. I put it together in the actual world. As a retail worker from Baltimore, I understand the challenges of balancing a demanding day job, managing fatigue, and maintaining the energy necessary to support my children.

If you're reading this while taking care of twin boys, a house full of in-laws, preparing for Thanksgiving, and trying to find the right Christmas tree, and you're doing it all with a helpful but tired husband, this is for you.

Being a parent doesn't mean having everything under control. It's about having the guts to attempt, the grace to stop, and the smarts to chuckle when things don't go as planned.

Thank you to my family for being there for me through the commotion and cheering me on every time I won.

This book is a reminder to all parents that you can do this, even when things are at their busiest.

With love and thanks,
Olivia Maxwell

Introduction

3 Days Is All You Need

Being a parent is a blessing and brings immense happiness to your life. It is a significant step forward. However, potty training is one of the few parenting milestones that makes parents feel excited, proud, and scared at the same time. Many parents experience a whirlwind of stress, doubt, and often unnecessary guilt during this process. The conflicting advice starts early, leading to self-doubt: "Wait until they are ready," "Do not pressurize the boys/girls," "Mine did not take much time. Don't know why your boys are so different?" "Your girl is too shy." "Be consistent." "Use rewards," "Don't bribe," and many more. I think I can even write a book on all the bits of advice I received. All these bits of advice can make the simple act of raising kids, specifically potty training, into a confusing psychological maze. Not anymore.

What if we could make this process less complicated? What if there were a clear, flexible, and truly parent-friendly way that was carefully designed to work with the realities of modern homes, the unpredictability of toddlers, and the demands of daily life?

Welcome to **Potty Training in Three Days.** This book does not make false promises of instant perfection. Instead, its goal is to help you understand your child's natural developmental pattern and to use a focused, structured, and story-based approach to teach them one of the most essential habits in life: using the bathroom independently in the morning.

Why This Book?

Let's confront the undeniable truth: contemporary parenting in today's world is a challenging task. There is no way you have time to read a 300-page instructions manual full of footnotes with your Zoom calls with your colleagues, boss, and clients; phone call with your parents and in-laws; while also undertaking your breakfast and lunch duty; or juggling an endless list of tasks before the day is over.

This is why this book is concise, easy to read, and carefully designed to fit into the busy lives of modern parents. Potty Training in 3 Days takes a lot of information and puts it all together, using:

- The relevant research on how habits form and behavioral psychology can help create helpful tips.

- Real-life stories from families with different needs that are real and helpful.
- Methods are carefully chosen based on age, gender, and personality, taking into account the specific needs of each child.
- The appropriate use of seasonality and time-of-day to help parents build necessary momentum at the correct times.
- The natural flow of stories that lets kids learn and spark their imaginations.

Introduction
- Purpose of 3-day taining
- Parent-friendly tone
- Blend of psychology, stories, and seasonal tactics

Foundations
- Day 1: Goodbye Diapers (morning routine, storytime)
- Day 2: Learning by Accidents (reset strategies, emotional pal pacing)
- Day 3: Mastery & Motivation (nighttime prep, reward rituals

Age-Based Strategies
- 18-24 Months: Curious Explorer (imitation, sensory)
- 2-3 Years: Power Seeker (autonomy, choice)
- 3-4 Years: Rule Learner (routines, gamification)

Potty Training in 3 Days
How to Ditch Diapers Without the Drama— By the Weekend

The 3-Day Plan
- Real Parent Stories & Wins
- Printable Tools (checklists, reward charts, tracker)
- Bonus audio stories + link section

Dealing with Challenges
- Setbacks & Travel (pause plan, portable kit)
- Personality-Based Tools (shy, stubborn, distracted, overthinker)

Real Life & Appendix

Our goal is straightforward: to help you and your child transition from diapers to dry pants in just three days, with confidence, clarity, and even a little bit of genuine fun.

Is It Possible in 3 Days?

At first glance, the idea of being able to potty train a child in just three days might seem like an overly ambitious marketing gimmick. But it is not. The "3-Day" idea is about using momentum.

When you spend three highly focused days with your child, making sure they are always prepared and actively participating, they will learn to connect the potty with feelings of success, comfort, and predictability. These three days mark a crucial starting point for a habit that, with subsequent gentle yet consistent reinforcement, develops into a natural routine.

3-Day Potty Training Journey

However, it is essential to note that "Potty Training in 3 Days" does not signify the end of the journey. Instead, it is the start of the journey towards independence from diapers.

- The goal of Day 1 is for the child to learn basic connections and recognize physical cues.
- On Day 2, there is a period of trial and error, becoming more aware of bodily signals, and

accepting that mistakes are a natural part of the learning process.
- Day 3 is all about practicing new independence with ongoing support and a structure that works.

After these three basic days, the critical phase of reinforcement goes on. This book will carefully guide you in maintaining this progress without losing your composure and momentum.

Every Child Is Different

You heard a lot: "Your boy should have started by now", "Why are you training your girl to be free from diapers? Isn't it too early?" and many more such versions. The idea of a perfect potty training age is a myth. A child's potty readiness is a complex mix of their personality, developing communication skills, emotional maturity, and even lesser-known factors, such as the seasons of the year. This book carefully divides strategies into groups based on this deep sense of uniqueness:

- **Age groups:** Providing tailored strategies for children aged 18 to 24 months, 2 to 3 years, and 3 to 4 years.
- **Differences between boys and girls:** pointing out what works better for boys and not for girls, and vice versa.
- **Temperament:** Giving specific advice to kids who are shy, strong-willed, easily distracted, or anxious.

- **Seasonal context:** including practical advice for dealing with winter problems, taking advantage of summer's benefits, and handling toddler life changes like travel or starting school.

You will also learn about strategies that work best at different times of the day, how to maximize your morning energy, how to utilize the quiet period after a nap, and how to use bedtime stories as powerful emotional anchors for learning.

Every child is different. So, instead of a strict or regimented framework, you will receive a flexible outline that can easily adapt to fit your child's needs and the needs of your family.

Expectations

This book provides a wealth of helpful information including:

- A meticulously crafted three-day schedule, complete with hourly suggestions, to ensure you remain focused and on track.
- The tips tailored to your child's age and gender, adapting to their growth and development stage.
- The schedule offering practical tools to help you maintain your sanity as a parent, ensuring you remain grounded and resilient throughout the process.

- Short stories that are fun, seasonal, and interesting, and that are meant to keep kids interested and help them learn.
- The practical solutions to common issues such as regression, navigation during travel, and overcoming fear.
- Easy to understand behavioral science made easy. So, expect no confusing jargon, but helpful, proven tools.

You definitely won't find the following things in these pages:

- Pushing or shame-based methods that make a child feel bad about themselves.
- Lots of theory that does not help you put it into practice.
- A prescriptive "one perfect way" approach that does not take into account how people are different.
- Lies about being a better parent or making false promises.

This journey is all yours, and you, and only you, are the best person to guide your child. We are only here to help you along the way.

A Fresh Start

You are about to help your child do one of their first big things on their own. This is a huge step. Yes, there will be times when things get messy. Yes, your patience may be pushed to its limits. Even though there will be problems, there will also be times of pure magic. You will see your child's confidence grow, their face light up with pride and realization that they are much more capable.

In just three days, things can start to change. Not perfectly, but enough to turn stressful times into genuine smiles and forgotten diapers into treasured memories.

Let's start this exciting three-day potty training journey together.

I

PART - I - The Potty Mindset

The emotional and behavioral framework using psychology and habits

1

Behavioral Psychology

Is It Only About the Potty

Imagine that, with a heart full of hope and excitement, you have just bought a brand-new, vibrant potty seat and have carefully placed it in the bathroom. However, rather than accepting it, your child looks at it suspiciously, even fearfully. They might scream, take a U-turn, run in the opposite direction, or perch on it only to jump off laughing.

Welcome to the complex and emotionally charged realm of potty training. This training accomplishes more than just physiological reflexes or muscle control; it delves deeper into a child's developing sense of identity, emotion, and power.

The Hidden Psychology

Potty training is not just a physical process for toddlers; it is a profound psychological transformation. They are being asked to give up something very comfortable and familiar, the diaper, for something unfamiliar, possibly emotionally frightening: the toilet. The following emotional triggers are also layered on top of this significant transition:

- **Pride:** Their growing sense of achievement, "I did it myself!"
- **Shame:** Avoidance can result from the sting of "I failed again," which can act as a strong deterrent.
- **Control:** The potty could become a battlefield as a result of the defiant "You can't make me" statement, which is a typical toddler assertion of autonomy.
- **Curiosity:** "What's this thing for?" demonstrates their innate desire to learn about new surroundings.

Potty training is often the first meaningful experience of autonomy for children at this critical developmental stage, as they actively build their sense of self. It can easily turn into a bloody battlefield for many reasons. The potty itself is rarely the cause of toddlers' resistance to using it. Protecting their fledgling sense of control is nearly always the goal.

"At this age, children yearn for independence. They feel controlled rather than independent when we push them too

hard with potty training." — Pediatric psychologist Dr. Talia Riven.

Habit Loops

The fundamentals of behavioral psychology show how deeply rooted habits are created by a recurring cycle of:

- **Cue:** An external signal or an internal feeling indicating an urge to leave.
- **Routine:** The acquired behavior, like actively using the restroom and sitting on it, and
- **Reward:** The favorable result that strengthens the practice, such as feeling clean, receiving sincere compliments, or receiving a physical sticker.

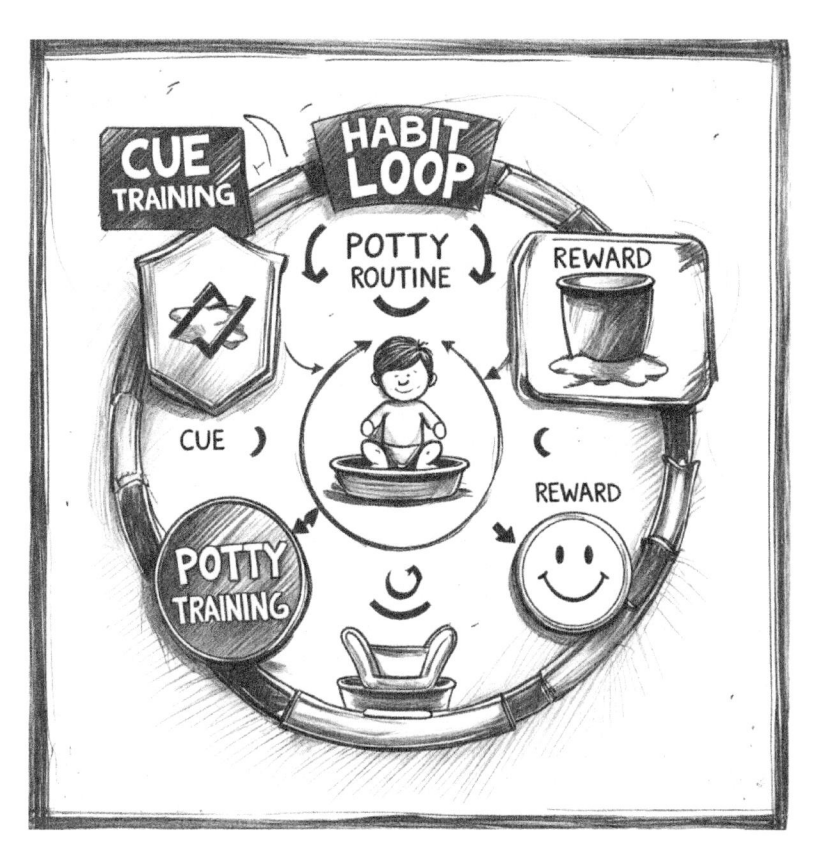

Habit Loop Diagram

The child's brain learns to connect the initial cue with the rewarding outcome through repeated practice of this loop. This learning mechanism is more effective for toddlers when the rewards are primarily social and emotional rather than merely transactional.

A simple bribe like "You will get a cookie if you pee" is far less powerful and effective than a statement like "You felt the tinkle, and you went to the potty! That is amazing!"

"Toddlers are wired for connection, not logic. Long-lasting habits are formed through emotional reinforcement."
— Behavioral pediatrician Dr. Karen Karp.

Incentives Reinforcement

Although positive reinforcement is unquestionably effective, it works best when it is connected to the child's proactive involvement and effort rather than just the result of using the restroom.

The overuse of bribes poses a serious risk of changing the child's internal motivation from genuine pride in oneself and internal mastery to a transaction or gain from outside sources. Without creating a reliance on tangible treats or a transactional mindset, verbal rewards, enthusiastic high-fives, and unplanned mini-celebrations are more effective in promoting repeat behavior.

Shame, Fear, and Power

Like adults, children also have an innate fear of failing. They fear disappointing the adults they love, and they hate creating a mess. Several potent emotional triggers can get into the potty training process through this innate vulnerability:

- If parents react to potty mishaps with annoyance, rage, or obvious disappointment, shame can quickly

develop. This adverse emotional reaction unavoidably produces strong avoidance behaviors.
- Toddlers' fear of the bathroom is a widespread emotion. Significant anxiety can be triggered by loud flushing noises, reverberating bathroom acoustics, or even the fear of falling into the toilet, and many more unknown reasons.
- The toddler's most potent tool is probably power. To establish their emerging dominance and control over the situation, they will frequently refuse to cooperate if they feel that you, the parent, genuinely want them to successfully potty train.

Never use terms like "Why did you do that again?" that can make them feel ashamed or frustrated. Use empowering and comprehensible language instead, such as "Oops, mishaps happen," "Next time, we will catch it," or "Do you want to try again right now or in five minutes?" This method creates a nurturing atmosphere that supports learning.

The key to successful potty training is using language that constantly empowers and redirects your child without causing embarrassment. Think about these powerful words:

- "Your body is brilliant, and so is your poop; it knows when it is time to leave."
- "Just like walking or coloring, learning something new is fun."

- "Don't worry. It's ok."
- "We will do it when you are ready."
- "Let's take a break and try again soon."
- "Amazing. You are growing. I see how you pay attention to your body. Mama and Daddy also do that! Wow! You are becoming independent!"

These well-chosen words successfully avoid the child's innate tendency toward resistance by subtly promoting cooperation and actively affirming the child's evolving identity. *"The secret is to repeat while maintaining emotional safety. Toddlers are uncertain, not resistant. Put safety first, not pressure."*

— Early Childhood Educator Emily Glaser.

Ava and the Magic Button: A Story

The intelligent two-and-a-half-year-old Ava was fascinated by buttons. When she listened to the subtle cues from her stomach, her perceptive parents cleverly explained that the potty had a "magic button," which only she could press. Ava's imagination took off, and she saw herself as a courageous space captain setting out on a vital mission.

Every successful "launch" of a trip to the bathroom was greeted with sincere joy and no pressure.

After a startling three days, Ava started actively asking to use the restroom, not because she felt obliged, but because she felt truly in control of her own little "space mission."

Jonah the Lionheart: A Story

Three-year-old Jonah was a fiercely independent child who detested being told what to do. He flatly refused to sit on the potty when his parents suggested it. When his parents realized how strong Jonah was, they one day converted the standard toilet into a "lion cave," and he became the courageous lion hunter.

They gave him a tiny flashlight to "hunt" for the lion sticker they had ingeniously inserted inside the toilet lid. Going to the bathroom suddenly turned into an exciting adventure. Every time he succeeded, Jonah would roar with pride, and whenever he told Grandma about his "lion potty" victory, he would beam with pure joy.

"Everything changed when we invited him to play a game instead of attempting to control him. He seemed to have picked up the skill of potty training on his own because it was enjoyable and convenient for him." — Jonah's father

Takeaways

- At their core, toddlers oppose what they perceive to be a loss of control. Children tend to pull back more

when their parents push them. Engage in positive, encouraging dialogues with your toddlers.
- Potty training represents a significant identity shift, transitioning from a state of dependency to one of increasing independence.
- Shame is a significant obstacle to their adventurous journey to take on new challenges. On the other hand, encouraging their curiosity propels their development.
- Compared to transactional physical rewards, emotional rewards, such as sincere praise, displays of pride, and group celebrations, are consistently more effective and create enduring habits.
- Regular repetition, a defined routine, and significant reinforcement are necessary for effective habit loops.

Keep in mind, "They are learning, not misbehaving." Gaining an understanding of these fundamental psychological concepts will help you potty train them more effectively and sympathetically.

We will move from the "why" to the "when" in the next chapter, discussing how to determine your child's readiness not only by age but also by observing the unmistakable cues their body and behavior are giving you.

2

Are You Ready?

When?

"When should I start potty training?" Undoubtedly, it is one of the most commonly asked questions by parents in early childhood development. A regimented response like "at 2 years old" or "only after they turn three" is an inaccurate response. Instead, the best answer is when your child is ready. Potty readiness is more about identifying and interpreting patterns in your child's behavior, physical development, and emotional cues than about reaching a specific age. Some toddlers may show obvious signs of readiness as early as 18 months, but others may not exhibit these signs until they are near their third birthday.

During this stage, your goal should be to observe rather than hurry. Children learn to control their bowels and bladder while also developing emotional awareness, verbal communication skills, and the cognitive ability to sequence actions. Due to these complex developmental interactions, early potty training often leads to considerable frustration for both the parent and the child.

"The goal of readiness is mental, physical, and emotional balance. You will encounter opposition if even one is out of sync." — Pediatric developmental therapist Dr. Lucia Grant.

Indications of Readiness

Many indicators provide a comprehensive picture of a child's readiness for this development and are applicable across all age groups. Review the detailed checklist below to determine if your child is exhibiting the holistic signs of readiness:

- **Remains dry for two or more hours at a time:** This shows that bladder control is growing.
- **Indicates when diapers are dirty:** This shows an understanding of how the body functions.
- **Exhibits curiosity about the toilet habits of adults:** Curiosity and imitation are powerful motivators for learning.
- **Able to follow directions in one or two steps:** vital to comprehending the toilet routine.

- **Pulls pants up or down without much help:** This indicates a growing level of independence and the development of fine motor skills.
- **Uses words, gestures, or facial expressions to convey the need to go:** This demonstrates a conscious awareness of the urge to eliminate.
- **Exhibits pride in achievements:** Indicates a drive for mastery and encouragement.
- **Exhibits interest in or participation in toileting habits:** a keen interest in the procedure.

It is time to move forward with a careful investigation through a readiness trial if your child routinely displays five or more of the above-listed indicators.

3-Day Observation Period

Utilize a highly focused 3-day observation method to gain in-depth insights into your child's unique pace and effectively eliminate guesswork. With this methodical approach, you can carefully record cues, identify reactions, and measure emotional responses without unintentionally putting undue pressure on yourself.

Day 1: Awareness

- Pay close attention to your child's current diaper habits.

- When they urinate in their diaper, do you see them halting, becoming quiet, or even trying to blend in? Look out for regular nonverbal clues, such as squatting, unusual silence, or specific facial expressions, that may indicate an impending bowel movement.
- Represent the toilet as a piece of furniture in a casual manner to set toddlers free from any pressure or expectations. Let it just exist in their surroundings.

Day 2: Interaction

- Offer the toilet seat gently. When your child is fully dressed, please encourage them to sit on it while doing something they enjoy, like reading a book or watching you use the restroom. Comfort and familiarity, not performance, are the goals here.
- Use open-ended inquiries to create interest without requesting a response, such as "What do you think this chair is for?" or "Does this look comfortable?"
- While reading aloud a kid-friendly potty story, pay close attention to your child's responses and level of participation. Avoid using any overt pressure.

Day 3: Trial Phase

- Start a brief trial period, roughly two to three hours, during which your child will not wear a diaper but

training pants or underwear so that they can feel wet as a result.
- "Do you want to sit on the potty before we go outside?" is a casual and non-demanding way to offer the restroom. Or "Before story time, let's try sitting on the toilet."
- Honor effort rather than results. Even if nothing comes of it, sitting on the toilet successfully should be considered a victory. Creating a positive association with the bathroom is the main objective.

"Given her age, we thought our daughter was ready at two. However, we saw no interest during the three days of observation. It only took three days for her to be ready after we paused and waited for a month. That observation period ultimately made the process extremely smooth and saved us a

great deal of frustration." The mother of a 2.5-year-old, Meera, Aanya

Age-Specific Readiness

Although the general checklist is generally applicable, distinct behavioral subtleties that tend to surface at various developmental stages offer additional insights into readiness:

AGE READINESS CHART

18-24 MONTH OLD	2-3 YEAR OLD	3-4 YEAR OLD
Starts mimicking parents, shows interest in the potty but has limited words to express needs	Loves asserting control—may say 'no' often, but shows signs of bladder awareness and can follow basic instructions	Enjoys structure, can stay dry for longer periods, and responds well to routines and social cues from peers
Curious Explorer	Power Seeker	Rule Learner

Age Readiness Chart

Ages 18–24 Months: Curious Explorer

At this age, a toddler :

- Starts to show that they do not like sitting in dirty or wet diapers. When their diaper becomes dirty, they actively tug on it or try to remove it.
- Exhibits a clear interest in watching parents or older siblings go to the restroom.
- May show early interest in the toilet but lack the self-assurance to use it independently.
- Uses dolls or stuffed animals to introduce playful potty interactions.

Ages 2–3: Power Seekers

At this age, a toddler:

- Starts using straightforward, basic potty terms like "pee," "poop," or "wet."
- Frequently hides to have a bowel movement out of privacy, then demands a diaper change right away.
- Take pride in their efforts to care for themselves and their growing independence.
- May exhibit the capacity to remain dry for prolonged periods, even during naps.
- May let you give them options: "Would you prefer to use the restroom before or after your snack?" or "Which would you prefer, your small potty chair or the big potty?"

Ages 3–4: Rule-Followers

At this age, a toddler:

- Exhibits a thorough comprehension of the toilet routine and the ability to adhere to multi-step instructions.
- Has the mental capacity to hold off on urinating for a short while.
- Starts to want privacy when using the restroom.
- Might exhibit symptoms of discomfort or embarrassment following mishaps.
- Might shows that peer imitation can work very well. You can use dialogues such as "Would you like to try using the restroom like your friend Maya at school?"

"A state of readiness is never merely physical. It is social and emotional. Consider more than just physical prowess when evaluating participation." — Licensed child psychologist Jenna Polanski.

Maya's Muddy Boots: A Story

Maya was a lively 22-month-old who loved to play outside and treasured her garden boots. Every time she had to poop, she would automatically run to a nearby bush, crouch down, and then proudly exclaim, "Done!" Her parents always noticed one particular habit. Her parents started the three-day observation after noticing this recurring pattern. On Day 3, under careful supervision, Maya moved organically to a potty chair placed in the garden and exclaimed, "No bush today!" Unquestionably, her readiness resulted from her observed behaviors rather than a fixed age.

Leo's Signal: A Story

By most accounts, Leo, who was approaching his third birthday, had yet to show any "obvious" signs of readiness. However, his perceptive parents observed a subtle but consistent pattern during their focused readiness observation: after snacks, he would discreetly withdraw behind a curtain to have a bowel movement, then come out saying, "Change." This one slight hint was crucial. Leo appreciated his privacy, and they knew he was ready. They turned the potty into a comfortable area by carefully designing a small, private reading nook around it. The recognition of his needs empowered Leo, and he was using the toilet on his terms in just one week.

"A lack of overt enthusiasm should not be mistaken for unpreparedness. When given enough room and confidence to learn at their own pace, quiet processors frequently achieve remarkable results."

— Early Childhood Behavior Coach Hannah K.

Readiness Chart

Every age group demonstrates distinct behavior patterns. These patterns help you understand whether your toddler's toilet is ready. The following charts offer an organized method for monitoring your child's readiness at various age groups:

18–24 Months

Behavior	Observed?
Watches adults in bathroom	Yes/No
Hides to poop	Yes/No
Pulls diaper when wet	Yes/No
Understands 1-step commands	Yes/No

2–3 Years

Behavior	Observed?
Says "pee" or "poop"	Yes/No
Stays dry after nap	Yes/No
Takes off wet pants	Yes/No
Wants to flush toilet	Yes/No

3–4 Years

Behavior	Observed?
Asks for privacy	Yes/No
Communicates needs clearly	Yes/No
Gets embarrassed by mishap	Yes/No
Stays dry for 3+ hours	Yes/No

Onward Journey

The journey of careful observation is where potty training starts, not when you buy a potty chair. Your potty training journey will be more profoundly successful and harmonious in the long run if you are more aware of and attentive to your child's distinct rhythms and subtle cues. Being ready is never a race to the finish line; rather, it is an invitation from your child to take part in a major developmental leap.

Since there is no one-size-fits-all approach, we will delve beyond readiness in the next chapter to explore how to effectively adapt potty training techniques for different age groups.

II

Part II: Tailored Strategies

Age-specific and gender-sensitive approaches for toddlers 18m–4yrs.

3

The Curious Explorer

Why is the 18-24 months Age range Unique and Difficult?

Toddlers between the ages of 18 and 24 months live in a world full of wonder and exploration. They are quickly becoming more confident in their walking skills, developing verbal and nonverbal communication skills, imitating adult behaviors with skill, and enthusiastically pursuing their growing independence. Experiments are ongoing during this time. Despite their rapid development, they have not yet achieved total conscious control over their bodily functions, though.

This chapter focuses on early-stage potty training, where exposure, rather than instant mastery, is the main objective. Your goal is to develop positive associations with the toilet, not to expect perfect results. Potty training works best for kids in this age range when it is presented as a fun routine rather than a strict, rigorous training schedule.

"Body awareness is just starting to develop at this age. We are promoting recognition rather than attempting to impose control." - Pediatric Neurologist Dr. Rina Kapoor.

Milestones in Development

Toddlers usually display a wide range of developmental milestones by the time they are 18 to 24 months old, which prepares them for early potty training. They:

- Walk with assurance and even try quick, brisk runs.
- Make use of 10 and 50 words while exhibiting a much higher level of spoken language comprehension.
- Consistently eagerly imitate the behaviors and actions of parents, older siblings, and even fictional characters on TV.
- Start to declare their independence, frequently using expressions like "Me do it!"
- Quickly react to straightforward, one-step instructions, demonstrating their growing understanding.

They are ideal candidates for a routine-based, low-pressure approach to potty training due to their concurrent cognitive and physical skills. This foundational stage enables them to start creating significant, long-lasting positive associations with the potty process, even if they are not yet fully trained.

Strengths and Limitations

One of the primary characteristics of many toddlers in this age range is their limited verbal communication, which is still in the developmental process. Even though they can't say "I need to go" yet, they have very keen observational skills. They are visual learners who respond well to clear visual cues, deliberate repetition, and regular routines. For toddlers of this age group, you should:

- **Employ consistent language:** Instead of using a variety of interchangeable terms, always use the same, straightforward terms, such as "potty" or "pee."
- **Combine potty breaks with interesting components:** Include short stories, songs, or gestures that are unique to potty time.
- **Set an example:** Let your child watch you or older family members or siblings use the restroom. This direct modeling is a priceless, fantastic learning opportunity.

"Pages, not paragraphs, are how toddlers learn. Building a dependable loop is facilitated by repetition in words, images,

and rituals." - Early Childhood Speech Therapist Kelsey Andrade.

Girls: Roleplay, Rhythm, and Sensory Play

Girls in this developmental stage often exhibit an innate propensity for pretend play and respond positively to gentle and predictable routines. For girls of this age:

- **Present a teddy bear or doll:** Choose a favorite stuffed animal or doll to "potty train" with your daughter. Have the doll sit on the potty and act like you are urinating.
- **Establish an atmosphere that is conducive to texture:** Make sure the restroom is welcoming and cozy. To minimize sensory discomfort, consider a comfortable rug, gentle wipes, and a peaceful, designated "potty nook."
- **Join in on a "pottysong":** Create or adopt a simple, catchy song to sing during potty time to add rhythm and warmth to the experience.
"Hooray hooray, it is pee-pee time! Come sit and sing and do your pee time." I used to sing this song to my Anna. You can develop your own Pee rhyme.

While she sits on the toilet, let her hold a small, soothing object, such as a security blanket or a favorite soft toy. The comfort and familiarity can significantly reduce any possible resistance or anxiety.

Boys: Visual Modeling, Sitting, and Story Framing

Randy and Kevin, my boys, at this age usually had gained a great deal from explicit visual examples and language that presents the task as a mission or a game. Boys of this age can be taught to:

- **Start with sitting on the potty:** Teaching boys to sit down for both urination and bowel movements is usually the best course of action at this age. Later, after their aim and balance have greatly improved, they stand.
- **Make a compelling visual observation:** Allow them to watch a parent, older brother, or even a kid-friendly cartoon character use the restroom successfully. It is frequently more impactful to see something completed than to hear directions.
- **Utilize mission-based terminology:** Present potty training is a commendable endeavor. It can be very inspiring to hear phrases like "Can you make a big splash like a pirate?" or "Let's help your underwear stay dry like a superhero!"

- **Training Method:** Using a small, floating target in the toilet bowl (such as a Cheerio or a small piece of toilet paper) as a "target" game is an entertaining and efficient way to transition to standing gradually. This gamified method enhances engagement and facilitates goal-setting.

"Boys frequently react remarkably well to gamification and challenges. Their cooperation and level of engagement can be significantly increased by framing potty training as an exciting

adventure rather than a chore."— Child behaviorist Jason Feldman

Awareness Building Activities

The following table provides examples of activities to enhance your 18-24-month-old toddler's journey towards becoming an independent potty-goer.

Activity	Goal	Example
Potty Book Time	Introduce visuals and words	Read "P is for Potty!" or "Everyone Poops" while sitting (clothed) on the potty.
Doll Potty Play	Role modeling and step sequencing	Show a teddy bear removing pants, sitting, wiping, flushing, and washing hands.
Dress-Up Practice	Transition from diapers to training wear	Use easy-on, easy-off pull-ups or soft cotton underwear for short periods, emphasizing feeling wet.
Create a Potty Corner	Establish routine and comfort	Set up a dedicated, inviting corner with the potty seat, books, wipes, and a small, comforting blanket.
Visual Steps Chart	Reinforce repetition and sequence	Create a simple, laminated chart with 4-5 images: Sit → Pee/Poop → Wipe → Flush → Wash Hands.

Emma's Potty Parade: A Story

Even though Emma was only 19 months old and only spoke a few words, she had a remarkable comprehension of almost everything that was said around her. Emma showed obvious, intense interest in her older sister, who had just finished potty training.

Her perceptive parents organized a fun morning "potty parade," in which a line of cherished stuffed animals joyfully made their way to their tiny potty chairs. Emma joyfully joined the procession, holding a colorful sticker chart in one hand and a potty doll in the other. Within a few days, she was enthusiastically cheering for herself while voluntarily sitting on her toilet (at first still wearing clothes). Three weeks later, she had her first successful dry morning.

"Nothing was forced. Emma's desire to participate in her big sister's activities was instinctive. Instead of making her feel under pressure, the 'potty parade' made her feel excited and included. That kind, lighthearted approach was crucial."
- Emma's mother

Oliver's Flush Fear: A Story

Except for the sound of toilets flushing, Oliver, a curious 22-month-old, was enthralled with every discovery. He was completely frightened by the sudden, loud noise. He would cling to his parents' legs and start crying every time they tried to sit him down, even close to the restroom.

An astute pediatrician made the brilliant recommendation to start by letting Oliver use a toy toilet. To give Oliver a sense of control, they got his favorite teddy bear a tiny plastic "mini potty" and let him press the handle over and over. Then, from a safe distance, they urged him to flush the actual toilet, cheering him on with loud applause each time.

Oliver conquered his fear in just one week. "Bye-bye, pee!" he exclaimed proudly as he flushed the actual toilet by himself.

"A strong remedy for fear is control. Toddlers' anxiety is reversed and their confidence is boosted when they are given agency and permitted to take the lead in the steps, even if they begin at the very end of the sequence, like flushing." — Child psychologist Dr. Sasha Lee.

Sensory Issues

Many toddlers object to potty time because of underlying sensory issues rather than outright disobedience. Taking care of these minor details can have a significant impact.

- **Cold seats:** Use a soft, padded potty seat insert to address this issue.
- **Loud flush:** Slowly introduce the flushing sound, maybe while soothing music or muffled background noise is playing. At first, some kids would rather flush from a distance.
- **Harsh textures:** Ensure comfort by providing extra-soft toilet paper or mild, moist, and flushable wipes.

- **Hard floors:** Provide a warmer, more secure footing and surround the potty area with a cozy rug and a non-slip mat.

Sensory Play Area

Give your child more control by allowing them to use easily removed stickers to adorn their potty seat. This sense of ownership transforms hesitancy into active curiosity and engagement.

Girls vs. Boys at This Age

Even though each child is different, the following general trends between genders are noted at this age:

Girls: They frequently flourish when using expressive language and engaging in creative pretend play.
- Have a propensity to enjoy making and adhering to routines (e.g., using coloring pages or sticker charts as part of the process).
- Often respond better to verbal praise and direct potty talk.

Boys tend to favor action-oriented language and describe tasks as games or challenges.
- Seeing other males, such as a father or older brother, use the restroom is a massive benefit of strong modeling.
- Frequently react favorably to proper equipment, such as visual aiming games or step stools.

"Never assume that potty training is easier or faster for one gender than the other. Boys frequently observe and process things deeply before they are ready to participate actively,

whereas girls may express their needs more vocally earlier."
— Pediatric researcher Dr. Elena Morris.

When to Pause or Reset

It is crucial to understand the pause or reset pit stops in your potty training journey. It is really important to know when to back off and avoid pushing too hard. Keep an eye out for these obvious pause signals:

- Abrupt panic attacks or violent outbursts, particularly during bathroom breaks.
- Even after extended periods of observation, there is no discernible awareness of wet or soiled diapers.
- Intense and persistent refusals to participate, despite gentle encouragement.
- Indices of discomfort or constipation that could be related to holding in.

Please take a quick step back if you see these signs. Give your child more hugs and comfort. For at least a week, avoid talking about the toilet directly. Following this reset, use only storybooks or lighthearted, non-threatening cues to reintroduce the idea gently.

Recap

- All interactions should be lighthearted and unhurried.
- Utilize visual cues, role-play, and regular repetition.

- Give much more credit to efforts than to specific results.
- Recognize that this stage is about laying the foundation and that complete training may still be months away.

Instead of treating the toilet as a burdensome task, treat it like a friend and an inviting tool.

Next Stage of Independence

The potty serves as a platform for a toddler to learn independence and is much more than just a place to sit. You are actively boosting their confidence without placing demands on them by regularly using songs, captivating stories, soft and reassuring voices, and small, manageable steps.

We will bravely examine potty training techniques for the age of developing willpower and emerging negotiation in the next chapter. This is the dazzling 2- to 3-year-old stage, when kids actively pursue power, push boundaries, and, ironically, still fervently want to be their hero.

4

The Power Seeker

Welcome to "Me Do It!" Phase

The 2–3 year period is unquestionably the age of assertion if the 18–24 month stage is best described as the age of imitation. Now, your adorable toddler has grown into a sophisticated little negotiator. Their vocabulary is growing exponentially, their emotions are escalating into strong, occasionally debilitating waves, and they have learned the enchanted, frequently intimidating word: "No."

The delicate art of training their developing will without unknowingly shattering their spirit is the sole focus of this chapter. Toddlers have an unquenchable desire for independence and, most importantly, control at this critical developmental stage. As a result, the standard toilet training may transform from functional to a frustrating battlefield.

However, with the correct strategy, it can become a transformative bridge to independence.

"Toddlers do not try to break the rules. They make decisions and try to fit in. They lean in rather than push back when you provide structure while remaining flexible." — Developmental psychologist Dr. Mallory Green.

Development Overview

Your toddler is likely to be displaying a wide range of new cognitive and emotional abilities at this energetic age, making it an ideal yet challenging time for potty training. Toddlers of this age are:

- Demonstrating a significant advancement in verbal communication, speaking in sentences of two to four words.
- Acknowledging their unique identity and frequently vehemently claiming it with expressions like "mine!"
- Beginning to express strong opinions about a variety of topics, ranging from their preferred activities to their attire and food choices.
- Gaining a basic understanding of cause and effect enables them to relate actions to their results.
- Struggling to regulate their emotions, leading to frequent emotional outbursts. They encounter "big feelings" such as intense joy, frustration, and anger.

These potent new emerging capabilities make your toddler experience a wide range of emotions. The secret to success lies in harnessing these emotions rather than letting it turn into an unrelenting tug-of-war.

Power Struggles

One of the first areas where toddlers truly discover they can use the power of "no" is frequent potty training. It can feel vulnerable to sit on the toilet. Giving up diapers' well-known security and comfort can often feel like a huge loss. Ironically, though, defying the toilet can also feel like a powerful way to assert one's newly discovered independence and acquire power. It is not defiance to refuse to urinate when ordered to do so. It is frequently a deeply ingrained emotional form of self-defense. They are defending their independence.

Strategically reframe potty time as a chance for them to take charge and feel empowered, rather than as a chore or something you need them to complete.

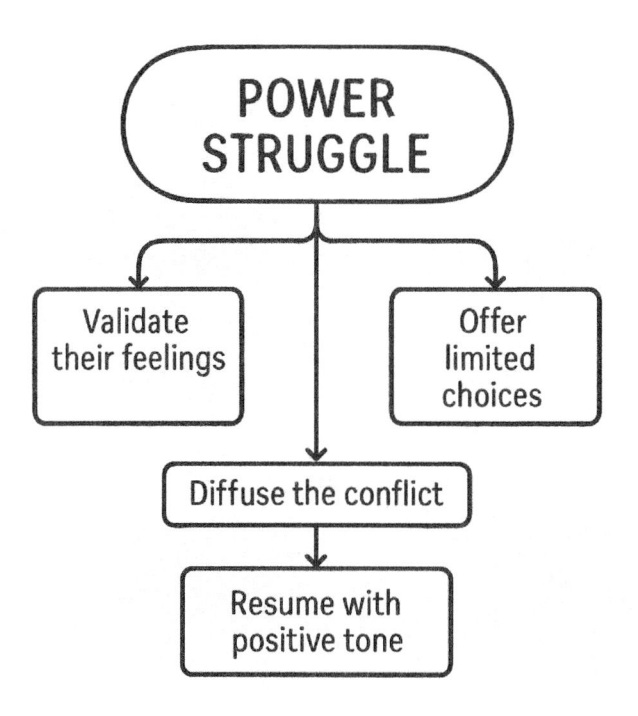

```
         ┌─────────────┐
         │    POWER    │
         │   STRUGGLE  │
         └─────────────┘
          ↙           ↘
┌──────────────┐   ┌──────────┐
│   Validate   │   │   Offer  │
│ their feelings│  │  limited │
│              │   │  choices │
└──────────────┘   └──────────┘
          ↘           ↙
      ┌───────────────────┐
      │ Diffuse the conflict │
      └───────────────────┘
                ↓
      ┌───────────────────┐
      │    Resume with    │
      │   positive tone   │
      └───────────────────┘
```

Potential power struggles can be significantly defused by becoming proficient in verbal rephrasing. Try these empowering substitutes:

- Give them a real choice by asking, "Would you like to sit before or after we read the story?" as opposed to, "You have to sit on the potty now."
- Rather than "No more diapers." try saying, "You are too big for that." "Would you rather wear your pull-ups this morning?" or "Let's wear your cool

underwear today?" This gives them a short-term option.

- Try saying, "I see your pants are wet," rather than, "Do not get wet again." That's how your body is trying to teach you. "Let's get dry together" emphasizes education and encouragement rather than humiliation.

"Control and curiosity are at the core of toddler motivation. They will naturally resist if they feel pressured. They will flourish if you deliberately give them a sense of competence and control." — Teresa Nash, Early Years Specialist and Parent Coach.

Girls: Fashion, Storytelling, and Praise

Many girls at this age show a strong receptivity to pretend play and place a high value on social approval. During potty training, take advantage of these innate tendencies by

- **Permitting her to select her underwear:** Allow her to choose her "big girl" underwear, flamingos or unicorns, to engage her directly. This tiny decision creates a great deal of ownership.
- **Converting bathroom time into a tea party:** Encourage her to throw her favorite doll, who also "needs to go potty," a tea party. Through play, this normalizes the act.

- **Honoring her decisions:** Give her specific and sincere recognition for her independent efforts: "The purple underwear you chose remained dry throughout the morning! Fantastic work!

Put together an alluring "potty fashion basket" with her favorite characters or patterns on it, complete with underwear and leggings that are simple to pull down. This gives her the confidence and excitement to transform herself.

"It is time to use the restroom, according to your doll's stomach." "Could you demonstrate to her how to sit and clean by herself?"

Boys: Challenges, Games, and Role Models

Games, races, and interesting challenges are often what boys at this stage thrive on. Make potty training an adventure and appealing by :

- **Presenting "Super Dry Pants":** Present his underwear as "Super Dry Pants," unique clothing that keeps him completely dry while on his significant "missions" and adventures.
- **Setting a timer: Make it an entertaining contest:** "Can you get to the bathroom before the timer buzzes and beat the beep?" This shifts the emphasis from parental nagging to a self-driven challenge.

- **You can expect male role models to be observed:** Urge him to watch an older brother, Dad, or Grandpa use the restroom. It has a profound effect to see crucial male role models model this.

Create a colorful "superhero chart." His favorite superhero receives a unique badge or sticker each time he successfully urinates or defecates in the toilet, signifying a triumph.

"Captain Clean Pants, are you ready for launch? Three, two, one, we're counting down. It is time to use the restroom!

"To stay involved and process information, boys frequently require movement. Transform bathroom breaks into brief, vivacious physical rituals, such as a hasty dash to the bathroom, a spectacular flush with style, and a joyous splash while washing your hands." — Toddler Behavior Analyst Greg Holloway.

Handling Tantrums

Tantrums are a common, if exhausting, part of a child's development between the ages of two and three, and the stress of potty training can undoubtedly increase their frequency or severity.

It is more effective to identify the emotion and then present two gentle, controllable options rather than trying to discipline through a tantrum, which can make matters worse.

Rather than a meltdown with sobbing or shouting, "Nooooo potty! I do not want to!" the parent said. "I hear that you do not want to go right now. It's okay. You can wait here for five minutes with your Teddy. We can try again." Now, which conversation would you pick?

To actively defuse the situation, use emotion labeling. Everybody gets angry sometimes. Let's take a moment before flowing with the outbursts and determine and act on the next course of action. This gently leads to a solution while validating the feelings of your toddlers.

Harper's Princess: A Story

At the age of two and a half, Harper loved dressing up. Harper's astute mother bought underwear embellished with tiny tiaras and let Harper use glittering gem stickers to personalize her toilet. Harper had the happy chance to "crown" her progress with a glittering sticker jewel every time she used the restroom, even if nothing came of it.

After accepting her role as the "queen of the potty" for four days, Harper woke up one morning completely dry and, much to her mother's surprise, ran to the bathroom on her own initiative without any encouragement.

"She had no trouble using the restroom. It turned into her throne. She didn't feel pressured or forced; instead, she felt totally in control and empowered. That change in viewpoint was crucial." - Harper's mother.

Jack: A Story

At the age of two years and nine months, Jack vehemently objected to being instructed. His parents faced persistent opposition until his perceptive aunt introduced the "Race the Flush" game. They eagerly let Jack flush the toilet while wildly counting down each time he was able to sit on the potty and urinate.

Jack loved the game and was completely engrossed in it. Before long, he started reminding them to "race the flush." They incorporated the potty into his already-existing world of games and challenges by ingeniously extending the use of the same timer to other transitions, such as snack time and cleanup.

Gameboard Monitor

"Jack's success was largely due to the deep sense of ownership the game gave him, not just the game itself. It was not the other way around; he was the one conducting the *ritual. This independence fueled his involvement."* — Family counselor Lila Forbes.

Choice-Based Resources

Let's dive into the table compiled on the resources required to achieve your goal.

Tool	Purpose	How to Use
Undies Basket	Fosters ownership over underwear	Let the child pick their favorite pair of underwear for the day.
Sticker Story Chart	Provides visual progress tracking	Each sticker completes a visual narrative (e.g., building a Pirate Treasure Map, decorating a castle).
Potty Timer	Offers control without nagging	Set for 45–60 mins; let them press "start" and "stop" to manage their own potty breaks.
Stuffed Animal Potty Partner	Encourages mimicry and empathy	Encourage the child to "teach" their favorite stuffed animal the entire potty process.
Song Cue	Establishes routine familiarity	Sing the same short, catchy jingle each time (e.g., "Potty Power!" theme song).

Typical Situations and Reframes

For the Power Seeker stage, it is essential to become proficient in these typical situations using deliberate reframes:

- The toddler says "No!" every time. Reframe it now and present two genuine, acceptable options: "Now or after snack?" or "Which would you prefer, the blue or the red underwear for your potty?"Resistance can be broken by lightening the mood. You could include

some humor. "What if there were marshmallow feet on the toilet?"
- "She might not tell you before leaving." Reframe it now and then gently prompt them right before their regular elimination periods. You could include connection and empathy. "Something is being whispered to you by your body. Together, let's determine whether it is time to leave."
- Sometimes, he hides in his diaper to go to the bathroom. Reframe it now, respect their right to privacy, and acknowledge it. You could include a solution-focused strategy. "Do you prefer to poop in your peaceful spot? To give you a private area, let's also put your toilet there."

"Children must understand that saying 'no' is safe." They paradoxically say "yes" more readily and cooperatively once that basic sense of autonomy and safety is established." — Child psychologist Dr. Denise Albright

Warning Signs

It is crucial to recognize the signs that your child needs a significant break from potty training, as they may be feeling overwhelmed. Be mindful of these warning signs:

- Increasingly severe and frequent tantrums follow almost every attempt to use the restroom.

- Deliberately withholding urine or feces until it causes obvious pain or discomfort.
- A reversal of other established routines, like irregularities in sleep, eating habits, or temperament.
- Complete refusal to participate, despite manifesting readiness on a physical level.

A two- to three-week break can help alleviate the pressure entirely if these warning signs appear. Please maintain current routines, read more potty stories, and offer general encouragement during this time.

Review

- **Provide authority through options:** Give them real constrained choices.
- **Employ storytelling and play:** Make it enjoyable by allowing them to use their imagination.
- **Incorporate role models, heroes, and dolls:** Provide your toddlers with dolls or toys of people with recognizable figures to emulate.
- **Normalize feelings:** Do not punish tantrums; instead, validate their emotions.
- **Give them credit for their efforts rather than their lack of effort:** Encourage them to try.

- **Take a step back when necessary:** Recognize that progress is not always linear and that breaks are obvious.

Next

Your toddler is actively experimenting with their independence rather than trying to test your patience with their claims of control. Potty training can become a place where power is shared, trust is firmly established, and you and your child leave feeling proud and successful if you have the correct resources and an understanding approach.

We will shift our attention to 3–4-year-olds, "The Rule Learners", in the next chapter and examine how they react best to routine, structure, and the inherent sense of accomplishment that comes with taking on new tasks.

5

The Rule Learner

The Young Child

A major developmental shift occurs by the time children are three or four years old, at which point the majority of them actively begin to crave structure and predictability. They are now actively involved in understanding norms, routines, and internalizing expectations, having progressed from the stage of purely haphazard exploration. Now, they have a natural curiosity about how things operate, a desire to achieve their "justice", and, perhaps most importantly, a strong desire to "do it right."

The 3–4 age range is a sweet spot for potty training due to this innate developmental tendency, whether it is the first successful attempt or a calculated re-engagement following a period of regression. Older toddlers are actively developing their self-confidence through observable success and mastery, rather than just learning the fundamental physical skills. At this point, it is your critical responsibility to provide them with tools that feel more like a simplified system they can learn to use rather than a tiresome struggle to be endured.

"Logic and consistency are beautifully received by children at this stage. They will jump up and take charge if you present potty time as a step-by-step procedure they can learn".
— Child psychologist Dr. Leah Crenshaw.

Why this Age?

Children who thrive in this age range typically possess a wide range of advanced social and cognitive abilities, making structured potty training relatively easy. They:

- Show stronger cognitive processing by being able to follow instructions with confidence in two to three steps.
- Improve scheduling by comprehending fundamental time concepts like "before" and "after."
- Seek adult approval and start comparing their accomplishments to those of their peers out of habit.
- Exude genuine pride in one's achievements, particularly those involving self-control.
- React favorably to acknowledgment and praise, especially when it shows their proficiency.

As long as potty routines are explicitly stated, consistently followed, and intrinsically rewarded, they are ready for self-regulation and often require few reminders.

Why Rules Work at This Age

Rules serve as an empowering roadmap for children aged three to four. They have a strong desire to know exactly what to anticipate, what behaviors will earn them a "gold star" or similar recognition, and what their peers are doing. This internal drive opens the door to incredibly effective tools, such as progress trackers, routine charts, and strategic reward systems.

"You are in charge of the potty routine now, what comes first on your map?" is a more empowering way to phrase the ineffective *"Do not forget the potty."* This small change turns a directive into a call to leadership.

Girls: Social Acceptance and Routine Responsibility

At this age, girls typically exhibit strong motivation towards peer imitation and a sense of accomplishment. Leverage these tendencies to help them on their potty training journey.

- **Encourage her to establish connections with their peers:** It is very inspiring to hear phrases like "I want

to show Grandma I am a big girl!" or "My preschool friends go to the big potty!"
- **Give her authority to lead:** Assist her in stating the standard procedures: "Wipe, flush, wash." This strengthens her sense of ownership.
- **Establish visual routines:** Utilize personalized charts with distinct visuals, checkmarks, or sticker stamps to visually record her achievements.
- **Ask her to "teach":** Encourage her to "teach" the potty routine to a younger sibling or a cherished teddy bear. This strengthens her comprehension and gives her more self-assurance.

"Girls' confidence in other daily tasks and routines is greatly bolstered when they feel capable and in charge of their process." — Early Childhood Educator Marion Levy.

Present the change as a unique "graduation" to the "big potty," similar to a particular preschool friend or her older cousin. This appeals to their need to fit in and imitate.

Boys: Task Completion and Gamification

When tasks are aptly gamified with a clear objective, a physical chart, and a hint of friendly competition, boys in this stage frequently flourish. To potty train your boys,

- **Make use of checklists, or points:** Implement a system in which participants earn points, or cross off items as they complete them.
- **Rewards as mission accomplishment:** Make accomplishments seem like rewards, like "earning his cape" by finishing a string of "dry-day missions."
- **Establish a basic system for potty badges:** Establish a potty badge system to let your boys earn one super badge for five successful attempts in the potty.
- **"Flush Hero":** He receives the coveted hero badge if he can wash, flush, and wipe his hands on his own without assistance.
- **"Dry Night Ninja":** He receives a unique "ninja" sticker after three straight dry mornings.

"Achievement systems directly address boys' innate desire for mastery and success. You will see much higher engagement if

you think of "mini-missions" as opposed to nagging reminders." — Child Behavior Analyst Logan Pierce.

The Potty Passport of Ava: A Story

Ava was a 3.5-year-old who loved to cross things off lists and was very organized. Her astute father made a clever "Potty Passport," a tiny, customized booklet with "destinations" like "Morning Pee," "After Lunch," and "Before Bed." She was rewarded with a desired stamp in her passport for every successful trip to the bathroom. Ava became so competent and independent in just two weeks that she was managing her toilet schedule and even alerting her father when it was time to get the stamp.

"Ava just wanted the satisfaction of finishing; she didn't want a traditional prize. She handled the entire potty process as though it were a significant undertaking that she was personally overseeing." — Ava's father.

Mason the Checklist Champ: A Story

Mason, a lively and energetic 4-year-old, had mastered using the potty at home, but at preschool, he showed perplexing resistance. His clever teachers collaborated to develop a "Bathroom Buddy Checklist," which the cubbies proudly displayed. Mason was able to check his box for the day each time he used the restroom successfully at school.

Four days later, there was a startling change: Mason eagerly ran to the bathroom at school before being asked, not just because he had to, but because he felt compelled to put his square on the visible checklist.

"Mason thrived on success that could be seen and the obvious, palpable proof of his accomplishments. In an area where he usually felt out of control, the checklist made him feel incredibly proud. It gave him more power." — Preschool instructor Ms. Tyler.

Potty Routine

The Rule Learner is directly appealed to by this organized routine, which is presented as a precise sequence:

Potty Sequence Chart

- Put down your work.
- You can use the restroom.
- You can pull down your pants and sit.
- Use the restroom (pee or poop).
- Clean thoroughly.

- Could you flush the toilet?
- You can use soap to wash your hands.
- Please be sure to keep your hands dry, and
- Could you put a sticker on your chart?

Repeat the entire process four to five times a day, even if your child does not feel the need to go right away. This regular practice strengthens the behavioral sequence and fosters deep confidence.

Reward Chart Templates

A sense of accomplishment is a bigger reward than the physical reward itself. Encourage your toddlers to display it with pride.

"I Did It!" Sticker Chart

Whenever they reach a milestone, encourage your toddler to pick up a pen and mark it with a check on their board.

Day	Morning	After Lunch	Evening	Dry All Day?	Stars Earned
Monday	☑	☑	☑	☑	★★★★
Tuesday	☑	☑	✗	☑	★★★
...					

"Potty School Graduation" Milestone Chart

Graduation day is always significant for all of us. Let's create a chart that shows key dates and progress toward self-independence for your toddler. Always cheer for their "Potty Graduation".

Milestone	Completed?	Date
Pee in potty without help.	☑	May 2
Poop in potty without help	☑	May 3
Dry for one whole day.	☑	May 4
Dry through the night.	☑	May 6
Wipes, flushes, washes alone.	☑	May 7
Helped teach someone else	☑	May 9

"You graduated Potty School!" appears after everything has been verified.

Overcoming Resistance

Even kids who are very structured can have moments of resistance or setbacks. Here's how to deal with such situations:

- Sometimes kids abruptly refuse to follow instructions even though they understand what is expected of them. Almost always, this is motivated by a need for control. "Your body knows when it needs to go" is a good way to persuade them. "Do you want my assistance today or your privacy?" This statement provides them with options, allowing them to make an informed decision.

- If they are afraid of using the restroom, use lighthearted, non-scary imagery in these circumstances, such as "Poop is just food your body does not need any more. It is ready to swim away and go on an adventure!" Give them authority over the "disappearance" by letting them flush and wave the poop off.
- At preschool, they regress. In such situations, create smooth communication between the home and the school. Create a small, laminated "potty card" or establish a shared reward system that accompanies your child, allowing them to track their progress in both settings.

"At this age, kids need to know implicitly that they can say no. Paradoxically, they say "yes" more readily and cooperatively

once that basic sense of autonomy and respect is solidified".
— Child psychologist Dr. Denise Albright.

Red Flags

At this age, readiness is typically expected. However, some warning signs should not be taken lightly. Consult a professional if your child exhibits:

- Constipation every day or consistently withholds stool, which may indicate underlying problems or anxiety.
- Severe phobia or anxiety, particularly about the bathroom or toilet.
- Frequent mishaps and regression after a prolonged period of mastering the process.
- Complete obliviousness and unconcern about wet or dirty clothing, indicating a lack of bodily awareness despite their advanced age.

It is best to gradually withdraw from active training in these particular situations or, more crucially, to speak with a pediatrician or child psychologist. Routine mastery is always subordinated to emotional safety.

Recap

- Make use of engaging charts, a clear structure, and dependable procedures.

- Make it possible to visually monitor progress using badges, passports, or checklists.
- Honor effort and increase accountability rather than perfect perfection.
- Ensure that the potty training plans at home and school are compatible and aligned with each other.

"This is about more than just rewards from outside sources. At its core, it is about creating a steady rhythm. Children's bodies naturally follow the learned routine from their brains once they trust the consistent pattern."

Drive Forward

When your child is three or four years old, it is not about how efficient they are in potty training, but more about how much of the process they can take charge of. You are becoming a facilitator instead of a director. Instead of giving them orders, give them the appropriate tools and structures, not embarrassment. After that, take a step back and observe the fantastic change that happens when they feel taking on new responsibilities as truly fulfilling and empowering.

The 3-Day Transformation Plan will be covered in detail in the next chapter, which will include an hour-by-hour structure, captivating narratives, and useful scripts to turn all this preparation and knowledge into self-assured, autonomous action.

III

Part III: The 3-Day Framework

A step-by-step guide for Day 1 to Day 3 with rituals, setbacks, and stories.

6

Day 1 – Goodbye Diapers

The First Day of the Rest of Their Potty Life

Today is a significant day because it is the start of your child's official potty training journey and your own path to fewer diapers, more independence for your child, and maybe even some tears (happy or sad).

Remember that the goal of Day 1 is not perfection. Instead, it is about total immersion. It involves planning a whole day that conveys that something novel, fascinating, and important is happening.

Confusion, curiosity, resistance, and even excitement are just a few of the emotions your child will probably experience, frequently all in the same hour. This emotional upheaval is entirely typical. They will use your composed, concentrated presence as an anchor to help them navigate this life-changing day.

"Pressure or force does not teach children consistent toileting habits. They pick up knowledge by identifying distinct patterns and feeling emotionally secure." — Pediatric developmental therapist Dr. Melissa Trent.

Focus, not Force

Recall, a perfect dry record is not our main objective for Day 1. Let's start paying close attention to the following patterns:

- When does your child typically get rid of things on their own?
- Are there any physical indicators or cues that they display?
- How do they react when someone sits on the toilet?
- Are they able to start connecting the internal drive, the physical action, and the favorable outcome?

In this section, let's deep dive into your hourly routine to make it happen.

Morning Setup (8:00–9:30 a.m.)

- **Bid Farewell to Diapers:** Create a mini-event out of this moment. "Today, we're saying a special goodbye to diapers and a big hello to learning something new and grown-up," is one way to phrase it. "You are

rapidly maturing, and I stand by your side". Celebrate every small step, and put a diaper in the trash or a special "goodbye diaper" box to enable them to participate actively. Give them a choice between two attractive pairs of underwear to further empower them. Let's participate actively in their new journey.
- **Setting Up the Potty Station:** Ensure the entire setup is soothing and easily accessible.
- An easily accessible potty seat or chair.
- Cleaners and an entire change of clothes.
- A cup of water and some nutritious snacks.
- Books with a potty theme or a little basket filled with interesting toys.
- A dry-erase board or sticker chart to record progress.
- **First Potty Attempt:** After breakfast, take them straight to the bathroom before letting them use a screen or play. It is acceptable if they do not urinate or defecate. You can hum a well-known song, read a brief story about the toilet, or sit with them. Finish with a positive statement: "Well done for sitting on your toilet!" That is the first crucial step.

Mid morning to Noon (9:30 a.m.–12:00 p.m.)

- **Strategic Hydration:** Serve water-rich snacks (such as slices of melon or cucumbers) and encourage frequent sips of diluted juice or water. This purposefully raises the probability that they will need to urinate, which also enhances their awareness of bodily cues.

- **Use the restroom every thirty to forty-five minutes.** Set an entertaining timer. Allow your child to hit "start" each time eagerly. Declare, "Let's see how your incredible body is doing. It is time to use the restroom." Always conclude with a compliment, even if nothing comes of it: "That was great sitting time. Your body is constantly learning and becoming more intelligent."
- **Pay Attention to Cues:** The following are typical indicators that a need to eliminate is imminent:
- Stopping or freezing suddenly in the middle of play
- Hiding, squatting, or becoming unusually quiet
- Pulling at their pants or the crotch area
- Saying "uh-oh" or looking down with a worried expression.

Say gently, "It appears that your body may be communicating with you, and if you notice any of these. Just in case, let's use the restroom together."

The Garden Fairy: A Summertime Story

Garden Fairy Story

"The Garden Fairy's wings glistened as she danced through dandelions and sunshine. However, oh! Her stomach started to feel queasy. She stopped and glanced around, wondering if it was time to locate her special flower seat. Then, in a magical forest, the fairy demonstrated to a squirrel how to use a petal-shaped potty. Similar to how your potty glows with your magic, it gave off a gentle glow when a squirrel sat on it.

As they sit on the toilet, read this out loud. After that, let them color a flower to "earn their glow."

Lunchtime & Nap Transition (12:00–2:00 p.m.)

- **Try Before Meals:** It is essential to establish a routine by consistently encouraging a bathroom break before lunch. If your child finds it easier to follow instructions visually, use a visual checklist.
- **Cues After Meals:** A bowel movement is frequently triggered by eating. Keep the toilet close at hand. Celebrate joyfully if they are successful in eliminating: "Your stomach knew exactly what to do, and so did you! High five!"
- **Preparing for naps:**
- If potty training is limited to the day, could you provide one last, mild potty cue?
- For their naps, use a pull-up, but make sure to refer to it as a "sleep diaper," highlighting its transient nature.
- Limit fluid intake about an hour before nap time if nap training is being used.

It is recommended to wear only underwear for naps and to use a protective mattress cover. "Potty, then pillow, the best nap will follow!" is the nap mantra.

Afternoon Play (2:00–5:00 p.m.)

This window is frequently the most difficult. Children's patience can wane because they are usually exhausted. But the lessons from earlier in the day are still being processed by their brain.

- **More Play in the Water:** Use cups, tiny pitchers, or a water table to involve them in water-related play activities. Drinking water can promote real-time learning and awareness by stimulating the bladder. "Let's splash, then dash to the potty for a quick check!" is a playful way to put it.
- **Mishaps Occur:** Keep in mind that mishaps are a normal, even beneficial, aspect of learning. React with composed, encouraging scripts:
- "It is alright; mishaps happen. We will try to catch it even earlier the next time. You are learning."
- "Your pants appear to be slightly damp. No issue! Together, let's get you comfortable and dry."

Never say something humiliating like "I told you so." That makes the learning process halt due to shame.

"A child receives a strong message when you respond to a mishap in a composed and encouraging manner: Your body is not 'bad' or shameful. More important than the immediate result are your effort and openness to learning." — Pediatric counselor Dr. Kayla Morris

The Snow Bunny: A Winter Story

"All morning, Snow Bunny played and hopped in the glistening snow. However, oh! Her tiny feet became cold, and then her stomach as well. She leaped back in and discovered her enchanted, warm seat, where tiny bunnies take refuge and comfort."

Then tinkle, tinkle!

Wrap your child in a warm, cozy towel to "be the Snow Bunny" after they have used the restroom. "The Snow Bunny felt warm and proud." This establishes a favorable emotional connection that is especially reassuring in the winter months.

Dinner & Wind-Down (5:00–7:00 p.m.)

- **Pre-dinner Prompt:** Gently remind them that dinner is almost ready. "Before we eat, let's give the toilet another opportunity to catch up." Try again soon after dinner if they initially say no.

- **Evening Sticker or Star:** Any accomplishment, no matter how minor, is worthy of praise. Give them credit for their effort: "Today, you truly paid attention to your body." That is precisely how champions pick up new abilities.

Bedtime Routine (7:00–8:00 p.m.)

- **The Last Attempt:** Include a "last potty" trip before putting on pajamas as a mandatory part of the bedtime ritual. Please encourage them to actively participate in hand washing, flushing, and wiping with little help.
- **Get Ready for the Evening:** Unless you are actively training at night, wear a pull-up or training pants. Present it in a positive light: Your body is still learning how to stay dry during the night, so this is only for sleep. You will arrive shortly."
- **Introspection & Calm:** "I saw how incredibly hard you tried today," you can say gently as they fall asleep. "Your incredible body will remember even more tomorrow, and things will become even simpler." You can also gently recite their favorite part of the day: "Do you recall sitting on the toilet after lunch? That was mature and courageous.

Typical Day 1 Challenges & Reframes

Just like any other day, each day is full of challenges, surprises, and disappointments, too. Please don't get disheartened, take it positively, and try to reframe your situation and your responses. Let's quickly take a look at it.

Challenge	Calm Reframe
"I do not want to!"	"Okay, would you like to sit before or after your yummy snack?"
Multiple mishaps	"That is perfectly okay! That is just part of learning. We're getting better!"
Refusal to sit	"Let's race your stuffed bunny all the way to the potty! Ready, set, go!"
Afraid of flushing	"Can you help me flush? It is a little loud, but It is completely safe!"

Learning has strong emotional roots, particularly for young children. You will surely see greater progress on Day 2 and beyond if you make Day 1 safer, more composed, and more optimistic." — Early Childhood Specialist Jamie Ellis.

Claire's Confidence Chair: A Story

At first, the large toilet intimidated three-year-old Claire. Her perceptive parents gifted her a little, padded potty chair that was lovingly embroidered with her name. Every time she sat on it, they sang a special "Potty Princess" song that they had written. It wasn't until late afternoon that Claire had to urinate, but when she did, she cheered and clapped so loudly that she started crying with happiness. Throughout the day, her parents placed the chair close to her favorite spot to play, providing a gentle presence instead of exerting pressure.

Claire made the bold and complete transition to wearing "big girl" underwear by Day 3.

Caleb's Timer Win: A Story

The highly active 2.5-year-old Caleb resisted receiving any direct instruction. Every half an hour, Caleb would eagerly "beat the beep" to the bathroom as his ingenious mother created a game using a kitchen timer. He missed the mark four times out of six on Day 1. But by the time he went to bed, he was actively racing himself.

Day Two? No mishaps.

"He required a challenge rather than an order. Everything fell into place once he had a sense of control over the game."
— Caleb's mother.

What Success Looks Like on Day 1

- Throughout the day, your child uses the restroom at least four times.
- Urinating using the restroom at least once, whether successfully or unsuccessfully.
- They show a certain amount of interest in the cues from their bodies.

- Throughout the day, there is no increase in resistance or fear.
- Throughout the entire process, you, the parent, remain composed, understanding, and supportive.

Thought: "You have already won a big battle on Day 1 if your child voluntarily sat on the potty even once during the day. "Celebrate that little step!"

A Habit is Planted Today

Although potty training cannot be mastered entirely in a single day, Day 1 marks the beginning of a vital brain mapping process. Through captivating narratives, your constant presence, encouraging remarks, and the development of dependable patterns, you have effectively established a lifelong skill.

We will strengthen and solidify these patterns tomorrow.

We will explore techniques for managing emotional setbacks, fostering healthy habits, and developing your child's body awareness without becoming overwhelmed in Chapter 7: Day 2—Learning by Mishap.

7

Day 2 – Learning by Mishap

The Mess

Day 2 is about the difficult but necessary process of navigating the unexpected, whereas Day 1 was mainly about novelty and introduction. This is the most crucial phase of potty training, when your child has a basic understanding of the routine but has not yet developed consistent self-regulation. And mishaps are always the result of this. Maybe a lot of them.

It is crucial to understand, though, that this is not a setback but rather a necessary and priceless component of the learning process.

"Mishaps are profound feedback, not failures. Toddlers learn by making comparisons between the fleeting discomfort of getting wet and the great sense of pride and achievement

that comes from a successful, clean potty trip." — Child psychologist Dr. Elaine Sawyer.

Parents frequently experience their strongest desire to give up on day two. DO NOT GIVE UP. Day 2 becomes the crucial link between early hesitancy and developing mastery, thanks to its steady use of soothing language, constant pacing, and genuinely reset-friendly attitude.

Expectations

You can better control your expectations and reactions if you are aware of the typical scene on Day 2:

- **More mishaps than on Day 1:** This is typical as they experiment with limits and pick up on subtle clues.
- **Potential opposition:** As they assert control, they might use phrases like "I do not want to!" more frequently.
- **A combination of advancement and regression:** There are flashes of inspiration interspersed with what seem like backward steps.
- **Higher emotions for both of you:** Both parents and children may experience emotional exhaustion as a result of this learning curve.
- **Developing body-cue recognition:** Before a mishap happens, you may observe them halting, reaching for their underwear, or displaying a specific expression.

To get used to the new routine, their nervous system is working hard. They are still working through the complex process of connecting their inner desires to the proper external response. Repetition and time are required for this.

Respond

Responding to every mishap with haste or annoyance is not the aim on Day 2. Your goal is to react in a way that continuously maintains your child's interest, curiosity, and, above all, emotional safety.

Your morning reset practice should include:

- **Welcome With Encouragement:** Get the day off to a good start: "You had a big day yesterday! Your body is discovering many fascinating new things. We get to practice once more today, which will help your body remember even more."
- **Emphasize victories:** Go over everything they did well on Day 1, no matter how minor it may have seemed. This increases self-assurance:
- **Encouraging prompts:**
- "That was fantastic that you sat on the toilet four times yesterday!"
- "You were so responsible to help me clean up after your pants got a little wet."

- "You washed your hands like a pro and flushed the toilet!"

You may want to bring back their narrative. Read the same seasonal tale (such as "The Garden Fairy Finds the Potty" or "Snow Bunny and the Warm Seat") again from Day 1. This repetition strengthens the positive associations and produces a potent comfort cue.

Scripts

Navigating the difficulties of Day 2 requires mastering these composed, upbeat scripts:

- **Floor mishap:**
- "Oh no, the urine leaked before we reached the toilet. That's all right! You are still figuring out where it goes."
- Try also, "Next time, we will try to listen carefully for that little tingle in your stomach."
- **If the children won't sit:**
- "Your body will determine when it is time to move. You can always use the restroom whenever you are ready."
- "Want to bring your favorite bunny to sit with you on the potty?"
- **After a mishap, the child appears embarrassed or distressed:**

- Try saying, "Everyone gets into mishaps, even adults, from time to time. I also had them as a child. Don't worry."
- "I am so proud of how you are trying your very best to learn something new. Look, Mama is so happy for you."

"Toddlers are susceptible to the emotions of adults; they frequently reflect what they observe. They will be willing to try

repeatedly if you maintain your composure, kindness, and patience." — Early Learning Specialist Rachel Feldman.

The Reset Routine

Please do not rush into cleanup after a mishap as though it were an urgent problem. Make it into a relaxing, mini-reset ritual instead:

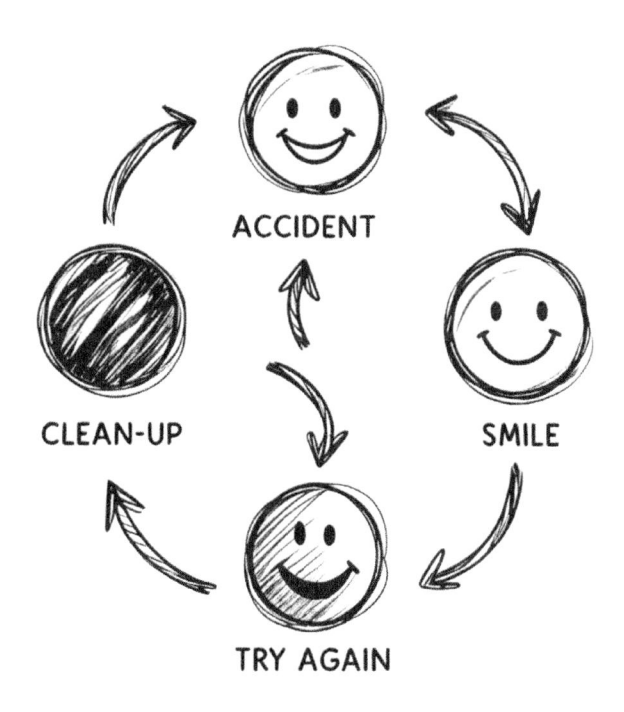

Flowchart for Reset

- **Speak in a steady, calm tone:** "Let's get cozy and clean again, sweetie."
- **Involve them in cleanup:** "Can you help me wipe the floor with this little towel?" is an example of a straightforward and doable task. "Can you put your wet pants in the hamper?"
- **Provide solace and a respite:** Offer a beverage and recommend a story you both enjoy. This removes the mishap itself from the scene and emotionally resets it.
- **Gently return to your routine: Encourage** them to try sitting on the potty again after they have been calm for 10-15 minutes.

Pacing Potty Trips

Your child's awareness levels may drastically change on Day 2, peaking with recognition and then falling into periods of distraction. Refrain from overcorrecting by requiring too many trips.

Try 45-minute intervals, but pay close attention to any subtle clues, such as:

- Crossing their legs or shifting uneasily;
- Staring off into space or abruptly stopping mid-activity
- Hiding or tugging at their garments

"Looks like your body might be talking to you," you can gently prompt if you observe any of these. "Are you curious if the toilet has a unique surprise in store for you?"

You can also try this. Train your child to maintain a "dry tracker" sticker chart. For each hour they stay dry, they receive one sticker. This increases their self-awareness and visually validates their progress.

Puddle or Potty?: A Rainy Day Story

The day was rainy and full of puddles. Leaping into mushy puddles was Finley the Frog's favorite pastime. Then all of a sudden, he froze! He pondered, "Was that a puddle, or was that ME?" Just in time, he jumped toward his comfortable potty log and exclaimed, "Whew! That was a close one!"

After reading, have your child do something. Allow them to assist "Finley" in making a choice. Ask which of the two toy frogs made it to the toilet the next time.

Sketch big puddles and a distinct picture of a toilet. Please have your child color the one that Finley ought to pick for his tinkle.

Leafy Larry's Fall Adventure: An Autumnal Story

"Leafy, throughout the entire tall tree, Larry was the most courageous and colorful leaf. The autumn wind swirled him down, and he floated gracefully, but oh! Abruptly, his stomach fluttered. In the garden, directly beneath his tree, he noticed a gleaming golden potty. "Just in time!" he exclaimed as he made a gentle landing.

Give your child multiple paper leaves that have been cut out. They get to add one leaf to the "Larry's Tree Poster" you drew on the wall for every successful potty use. This creates a graphic depiction of their achievements.

Lily's Dance Floor Mishap: A Story

Three-year-old Lily was dancing happily to her favorite song when she froze and, much to her surprise, peed on the carpet. She was so embarrassed that she started crying right away. "It is okay, sweetie," her understanding father said, kneeling and giving her a tight hug. Your body is picking up new skills. It just works things out like this. Not a huge deal.

They played her favorite song again ten minutes later, and during the chorus, they subtly encouraged her to take a bathroom break. They soon adopted this rhythmic association as a reliable cue. By Day 3, Lily was running to the bathroom with assurance before her song had even reached the halfway point.

"She required routine and rhythm that she could relate to." Her body remembered what we praised and made positive, as well as what we cleaned up.

Henry's Hide-and-Seek: A Story

On Day 2, 2.5-year-old Henry started hiding behind the couch whenever he had to poop. Instead of reprimanding him, his wise parents quietly carried the toilet to his favorite hiding place and said, "This location is ideal if your body needs quiet to urinate. You are welcome to sit here by yourself."

Two days later, on Day 4, Henry was successfully urinating in the potty directly behind the couch and proactively calling out, "I am hiding!"

"Sometimes, kids are just defending their intense need for privacy and bodily control, not the toilet itself. Meeting that need can lead to quick advancement." — Pediatric Behavior Specialist Dr. Kay Morrison

Handling Refusal

If you notice these critical indicators of non-cooperation:

- Your child spends an entire afternoon refusing to sit on the potty.
- They have three or more consecutive mishaps without making any successful trips to the bathroom.
- When the topic of potty time is brought up, they frequently cry or exhibit severe distress.

Don't overreact. Hold on. Let's try this.

"Looks like potty time is not feeling fun right now" is a precise, reset phrase that can be used. "Let's put it out of our minds for a bit and return when we feel better." Take a 30- to 60-minute break without being asked. Give hugs, read a favorite story, or take a cool stroll outside. Use a playful, low-pressure approach to gently re-engage after this reset.

Allow your child to "potty train" a doll or action figure while you are taking a break. As a result, they can process the steps without experiencing immediate pressure.

Evening Motivation (5:00–8:00 p.m.)

"You are learning something incredibly new and important, and that always takes practice," is a calm recap that can be done during dinnertime. "You are making a fantastic effort."

Before putting on your pajamas, give them one last chance to use the restroom and provide them with a lot of praise for trying: "You worked hard before bed. That's precisely what older children do."

Read their favorite story from Day 2 (Leafy Larry or Puddle or Potty) to cap off the evening. Finish with a heartfelt statement: "Your incredible body will remember even more tomorrow. I'm so proud of you for trying so hard today."

What Success Looks Like on Day 2

They are aware of or react to their body's signals, albeit erratically.

- Throughout the day, they voluntarily attempt to sit on the toilet several times.
- Although they might show some resistance, they usually stay involved in the process.
- They can successfully use the restroom one to two times, even if it is only for a single drop.
- They take pride in at least one minor accomplishment.

You should be genuinely proud of their efforts.

"I Tried Today" Reflection Chart

On Day 2, you should reflect on your reactions to various situations to track your emotional progress, too.

Time	What Happened	How I Felt	What I Did Next
9 AM	Sat but didn't pee	Happy	Got a sticker
11 AM	Peed in pants	Sad	Cleaned with Mom
1 PM	Peed in potty	Proud	Gave a high five
6 PM	Refused potty	Mad	Read a story

Let your child express their feelings by coloring a box or drawing a face. Alongside their developing body awareness, this small action heightens their emotional awareness.

From Mess to Mastery

Rarely is potty training a straight line. Day 2 is a critical stage of profound reinforcement and consolidation, even though it frequently feels like a time of frustrating regression. Your child will be empowered to take the next essential steps with unwavering confidence once they understand that mistakes do not carry shame, thanks to your composed and consistent responses.

We will build on today's progress in Chapter 8: Day 3- Mastery and Motivation, where your child will embrace dry pants, beam with big smiles, and celebrate every success, making them feel like the victorious hero of their own story.

8

Day 3 – Mastery and Motivation

From Learner to Leader

It usually starts to "click" on day three. This change does not occur because mishaps suddenly stop happening, although you will likely notice a decrease in mishaps; instead, it happens. After all, your child begins to feel a strong sense of pride and responsibility.

Your child will transition from being a passive participant to an active owner and leader of their toilet journey on this crucial day. Like little superheroes, they will begin to ask to use the restroom actively, consistently recognize their body's cues, and maybe even proudly announce their accomplishments.

"The primary force behind mastery is empowerment. Children start doing things, not just once, but repeatedly and with confidence, when they genuinely think they can succeed."
— Pediatric behavioral specialist Dr. Serena Pike.

On Day 3, your role is still straightforward but crucial:

- Give sincere, targeted praise to reinforce accomplishments.
- Encourage them by praising their developing skills.
- Give them as much control over the procedure as you can.

Follow the Process

On Day 3, getting perfectly dry pants isn't our only goal. We are actively raising a child who:

- Recognizes and responds to their body's signals.
- Take immense pride in their work and endeavors, regardless of the immediate results.
- Possess the ability to laugh off mistakes gleefully and willingly, and try again without any sense of guilt.

Morning Momentum (7:30–9:30 a.m.)

Celebrate Victories:

- Suppose your child is dry when they wake up: "Whoa! Throughout the night, your body stayed dry,

and you slept well. That is simply incredible! You truly are a champion at night."
- If not: "That's fine. Our bodies have a lot of work to do at night. As we proceed, we will teach your body how to stay dry overnight."

Review Their Journey:

- Pause, review, recognize, and express the progress they have made in just two days:
- "Remember, yesterday you weren't aware how to sit on the toilet? Look at you now. Now you are confidently using the toilet every time! Good job!"
- "You have been learning so much, picking your underwear, and helping clean up."
- Encourage active participation by having them draw stars for each successful try or attempt, or by sticking stickers on a noticeable "Potty Hero" chart.

Buzz the Bee: A Spring Story

"Buzz the Bee spent the entire day consuming sweet nectar while joyfully hopping from vibrant flower to vibrant flower. However, oh! Buzz's stomach began to wiggle a little. He knew exactly what to do! Just in time, he landed gracefully on the unique "Potty Petal" and exclaimed, "Bee-tastic!" In celebration of Buzz, the entire garden clapped its leafy hands.

Give your child a sticker of a bee after they have finished reading. On a poster or a sketched image, they get to "fly" their bee sticker to their toilet each time they successfully use it.

Midday Mastery (10:00 a.m. – 2:00 p.m.)

During this crucial period, you have the opportunity to empower them to take charge and genuinely steer the process.

- Play the game of "reverse mentoring" by having your child "teach" a cherished stuffed animal or toy how to use the restroom:
- "Teddy is unsure of where to use the restroom. Can you demonstrate exactly what to do for him?" Encourage them to describe the procedure out loud, going over each step.
- Let them act out tasks for their toy, such as flushing or wiping. This act of instruction and imitation gives them a great sense of empowerment.

"Teaching by nature reinforces mastery." A toddler is actively creating and strengthening their internal mental model of the process when they are given the chance to teach a toy." — Early Childhood Educator Dr. Laura Menen

- **Anchors of Confidence:** For their success, create and recite short, empowering mini-mantras. Encourage them to say, "I can go potty confidently!"

- "My body knows just what to do!" "Oops means I am learning, and that is okay!"

As a visual reminder of their development, let them sketch their favorite triumphant moment from Day 1 or Day 2 and proudly hang it next to the toilet.

Santa's Potty Pass: A Holiday Story

Santa's Potty Pass

"Santa felt a little 'uh-oh' in his stomach as he was busy double-checking his list and getting ready for his big Christmas Eve ride. "There's no time to waste!" he laughed, leaping from his sleigh and into a festive potty that was decorated with candy canes. "Even Santa knows: potty before cookies and flying!" exclaimed Mrs. Claus.

Have fun.

As Santa gets his reward before his big journey, give your child a special "Potty Pass" coupon that they can use to get a high five, a particular sticker, or a celebratory hug every time they try or succeed at using the potty!

Late Afternoon: Locking It In (2:00–5:00 p.m.)

You can use this time to establish their developing potty-predicting skills.

- **Create a chart of body clues:** Make a mini-poster together. "How Does My Body Tell Me It is Time?" is the title. Make use of words that your child can relate to, such as "I wiggle when I need to go" or "I stop dancing or playing." Or "My stomach feels funny."

Allow them to illustrate each clue with a little picture or a basic emoji.

- **Introduce Potty Challenges:** Offer a playful "Potty Hero" badge to competitive kids, which is often popular among boys. When they reach milestones like three hours without urinating or successfully "catching" a pee after consciously recognizing the urge themselves, they are awarded this badge.

Evening Rituals & Bedtime Prep (5:00–8:00 p.m.)

The foundational habits for nighttime dryness start now, even though it is usually a longer-term developmental goal.

- **Pre-Bed Wind Down:** As part of their soothing bedtime ritual, encourage one final, gentle bathroom visit: "Let's help your body relax and get ready for sleep." Potty, then pajamas, and finally, warm embraces. Give them autonomy by allowing them to wash their hands and flush independently with minimal assistance.
- **Frame the Night:** To establish positive expectations for the evening, use the following positive language: "Our bodies can be so intelligent that they will occasionally wake us up in the middle of the night to use the restroom. Keep in mind that your toilet is nearby if you experience that." If they aren't yet using the adult toilet on their own, ensure the nightlights are on and keep the potty seat nearby.
- "These are just your special sleep pants for now, to help keep your bed dry until your amazing body tells us it is completely ready to stay dry all night all by

itself" is a positive way to frame pull-ups if you are still using them overnight.

Lucy's Lemonade Stand: A Story

On Day 3, Lucy, who was 2.5 years old, was having trouble staying consistent, and her motivation was waning. Her parents came up with an ingenious solution: a miniature "potty lemonade stand." Lucy received a dummy coin each time she managed to use the restroom. She was then entitled to a fun straw and a real, refreshing cup of lemonade after earning five coins.

By the evening, Lucy was sincerely inspired by the game and was trying every 30 minutes. "She felt so in control," her mother noted. She connected with achievement-based play rather than bribery.

Ben's Big Brother Boost: A Story

At three years old, Ben showed little interest in potty training at first. Josh (6), his older brother, stepped in as a strong motivator. Josh created the "Potty Champion Club." Ben was told that he could only become a member of this exclusive club if he showed Josh and a few stuffed animals how to use the toilet properly.

By Day 3, Ben had joined the Potty Champion Club and, thanks to his newly acquired skills, had even proclaimed himself its "president."

"For toddlers, peer motivation, even from an older sibling, is frequently far more potent and successful than just explicit adult praise." — Family Therapist Kelsey Morgan.

Final Day 3 Checklist

Have they…

- Decided to go alone at least once without being specifically asked?
- Successfully urinate or defecate two or three times?
- Accurately reacted to at least one body cue, such as pausing or uttering "uh-oh"?
- Flushed or cleaned up with apparent assurance and less help?
- Employed affirming expressions regarding the act of using the restroom, such as "I did it!" and "Potty time!"

Awoke with a sense of calm or excitement at the thought of carrying on with their toileting journey?

Printable "I Did It!" Certificate Template

You can create a personalized, joyful reward using your child's name:

This certificate celebrates **[Child's Name]**

For completing Potty Training in 3 Days!
You listened to your body, tried your best, and became a true Potty Pro!

Date: _____ **Signed by:** _____

Let them actively participate in decorating it with crayons or stickers, and then proudly display it in a prominent location.

Transformed, Not Just Trained

Completing potty training in three days does not guarantee flawless results or eliminate all mishaps. It represents three days of deep empowerment and fundamental knowledge.

You have successfully taught them basic body awareness, instilled a great deal of confidence in their skills, modeled essential emotional safety throughout the learning process, and established a happy and encouraging learning environment.

There may still be the odd mishap tomorrow. That's a regular part of the longer journey. But today, you have established a foundation that is far more valuable and robust than any sticker chart: trust in yourself and your direction.

Next Up: Maintenance Week—The Next Seven Days

We will go beyond the rigorous 3-day approach in the next chapter and explore practical tactics for establishing long-lasting, stress-free daily routines. This includes essential adjustments for daycare and preschool settings, handling visits to grandparents' homes, and skillfully navigating any regressions that may occur during illness or significant life transitions.

IV

Part IV: Troubleshooting

Navigate regressions, tricky personalities, and emotional setbacks with calm

9

Beyond Three Days

Overcome Setbacks

You have completed three concentrated days of rigorous potty training. This must be an emotional roller coaster ride, with many ups and downs. I am sure you have enjoyed it and made significant progress. You may have seen some incredible victories as your child proudly wipes their hands like an experienced adult, runs to the toilet with confidence, or cheers with unrestrained joy as they flush.

Then, suddenly, your child regresses to their prior behavior pattern and stubbornly refuses to participate in potty time for the whole day. Perhaps someone discreetly has a bowel movement behind the couch, a behavior once thought to be extinct.

It is essential to realize that it is not a failure. Instead, it is a strong signal. It is your child's natural way of saying, "I need help understanding or coping with this change."

"When faced with new stressors, significant transitions, or rapid growth spurts, children often revert to their previous behaviors, which is a type of emotional regression known as potty regression."

— Developmental psychologist Dr. Lillian Pace.

The Triggers

Multiple reasons often trigger such regressions. This is a typical healthy stage of development. You can handle it more skillfully if you comprehend these triggers. Typical regression triggers are:

- **The arrival of a new sibling:** A significant change in the focus and dynamics of the family.
- **Beginning preschool or daycare:** A new routine, setting, and social expectations.
- **Relocation or travel:** Upsetting routines and familiar surroundings.
- **Illness, constipation, or medication:** Modifications in body function or physical discomfort.
- **Modifications to the routine or caregivers:** A change in the day's schedule or the person providing the care.

- **Parental stress or significant life events:** Kids are susceptible to their parents' feelings and affected by events happening in their lives, including, but not limited to, divorce, death in the family, job loss, excessive alcohol or other drug consumption, and accidents.

Symptoms :

- Disregard for prior cooperation.
- Sudden increase in mishaps after a period of dryness.
- Hiding to urinate or defecate is a habit rooted in their previous diaper-wearing behavior. After transitioning to underwear, they request diapers again.
- Children may cry or whine to show distress, especially during potty time.

These symptoms are not comprehensive and may include other deviations from previous cooperative behavior as well. It has been observed that in the face of perceived instability or stress, regression often serves as a cover for a more profound need - a need for comfort, control, or assurance.

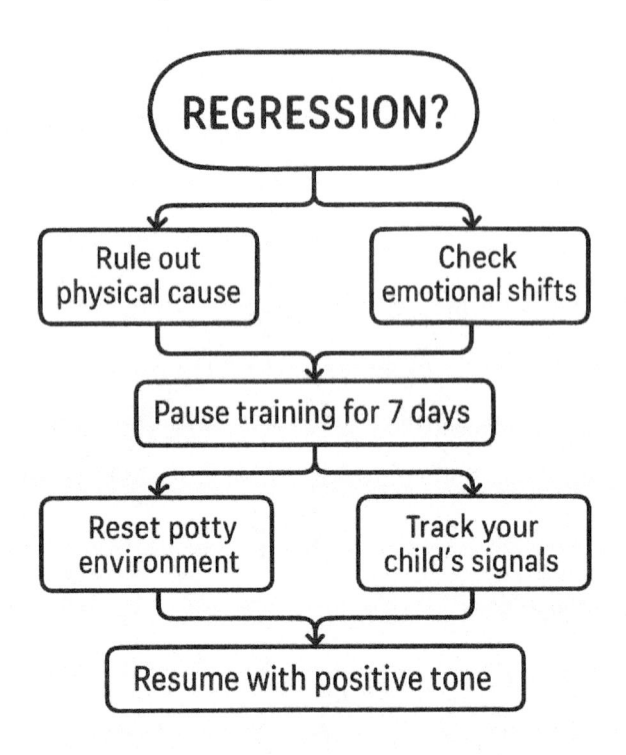

```
                    ┌─────────────┐
                    │ REGRESSION? │
                    └─────────────┘
                      ↙         ↘
          ┌──────────────┐   ┌──────────────────┐
          │   Rule out   │   │      Check       │
          │physical cause│   │ emotional shifts │
          └──────────────┘   └──────────────────┘
                      ↘         ↙
                ┌──────────────────────┐
                │ Pause training for 7 days │
                └──────────────────────┘
                      ↙         ↘
          ┌──────────────┐   ┌──────────────┐
          │ Reset potty  │   │  Track your  │
          │ environment  │   │child's signals│
          └──────────────┘   └──────────────┘
                      ↘         ↙
                ┌──────────────────────────┐
                │ Resume with positive tone │
                └──────────────────────────┘
```

Regression Decision Matrix

Your Reactions

When dealing with such regression, it is essential to maintain a composed, inquisitive, and connected attitude. Your response influences their reaction. In such regression instances:

Avoid:

- Shame them or discipline them if your child has a mishap.
- Convey disappointment or annoyance with expressions like "I thought you were done with this!" or "You are a big boy/girl now, why did you do that?"
- Comparison with others: "Your cousin no longer has mishaps."

Do:

- Empathically acknowledge their emotions by saying, "It seems like your body is feeling a little confused today, and that is okay."
- Provide consolation and connection by saying, "Let's cuddle for a while. Do you want to talk about what happened there or maybe later?"
- Gently reiterate and reestablish the routine: "We are going to assist your body in relearning how to use the restroom. Together, we can accomplish this."

"Toddlers are subtly asking you to get back on their emotional level when they regress. That is the exact point at which real

growth, based on comprehension and encouragement, resumes." — Family Therapist Camille Roth.

The 7-Day Pause & Reset Plan

When regression persists for an extended period, taking a calculated step back is the best course of action. Use this structured 7-day reboot plan if regression persists for longer than 3–4 days and potty training becomes a constant struggle.

Day 1–2: Complete Emotional Recovery

- Return to using diapers or pull-ups without embarrassment or criticism. Present it as a short-term comfort measure.
- Unless your child mentions it explicitly, refrain from discussing the potty.
- To lower overall stress, give your full attention to play, connection, and upholding other accustomed routines.

Day 3–4: Gentle Reintroduction

- Reintroduce materials with a potty theme gradually. Together, read potty books in a comfortable environment.
- Let your child "potty train" their favorite toys or dolls by giving them practice.
- Reaffirm positive memories by casually discussing their prior potty successes.

Practice potty play on days five and six.

- Allowing them to choose unique "potty clothes" (such as easy-on, easy-off underwear) or decorate the potty with detachable stickers will empower them.
- Promote one brief sit per day, completely voluntary, after meals or at other regular times.

Day 7: Calm Re-engagement

- Start a one-day at-home toilet refresh, reverting to the rigorous Day 1 techniques, but using a more relaxed approach.
- Throughout the day, consistently use confidence-boosting techniques and positive language.

When you implement a reset, you are not starting anew. By relieving stress and restoring your child's confidence, you are essentially reestablishing a connection with their natural readiness rhythm.

Logan's Preschool Diversion: A Story

Three-year-old Logan was intelligent and completely potty trained at home. But he started wetting his pants twice a day when he started preschool. His parents were initially irritated when they discovered the classroom restroom was located in a chilly, poorly lit corner, an atmosphere that likely made them feel uneasy.

A "potty buddy basket" with intriguing books and a tiny flashlight was placed next to the toilet by his perceptive teacher, who recognized the underlying fear. Within 48 hours, Logan was able to resume using the restroom successfully thanks to this reassuring addition.

The environment is critical. Occasionally, we interpret a child's "I won't" as a silent cry of "I am scared." The key is to address the emotional or environmental barrier.

On The Go Potty Training

Whether it is a quick weekend trip to Grandma's house or a cross-country flight, travel always challenges routines. However, with careful planning and considerable patience, you can transform it from a potential "wipeout" into a fruitful educational experience.

Essential Travel Potty Kit: When planning to travel, ensure your potty kit is ready to avoid inconvenience and embarrassment. It should have:

Portable Potty Kit

- **Portable Potty Seat:** A foldable or travel-sized potty seat for added convenience.
- **Wipes & Extra Clothes:** For fast cleanups and a change of clothes.
- **Storybooks & Flashcards:** Comfortable visual aids and well-known stories with a potty theme can facilitate transitions and offer solace in unfamiliar situations.

- **Potty Backpack:** Give your child a small backpack to carry their necessities, such as a special potty toy, a small reward chart, and their favorite underwear. This encourages accountability and enthusiasm.

"My daughter felt more responsible and eager for our trip rather than nervous when they packed their toiletries. She had a special "travel potty kit." — Mandy G., Mom of Two.

Miles & the Magical Airport Potty: A Story

"Miles was giddy with anticipation for his first flight on an airplane! Oh no! The signs all looked different and confusing when they arrived at the airport restroom. "This is our magical potty; it hears when you say the magic word!" said a smiling, helpful airport attendant. The potty seemed to sparkle exclusively for Miles when he whispered, "Tinkle Time." Feeling brave and ready for his big adventure, he laughed and walked with pride.

Create a unique "Potty Passport" for your child. Each time they successfully use the restroom in a new or unfamiliar location—like Grandma's house, a restaurant, an airplane, or a hotel—they earn a stamp (sticker) in their passport. This approach makes travel potty training more enjoyable.

It Is Time To Reboot

Minor regressions are standard, but occasionally, a more thorough pause and restart are required. If your child exhibits the following symptoms and the regression persists for more than 11-12 weeks without showing any signs of improvement, it's time for a complete reboot:

- Your child consistently rejects all attempts to use the restroom.
- They display overt signs of discomfort or fear, such as crying, clenching, or severe anxiety, which are specifically associated with the toilet.
- They start to withhold things, particularly when it comes to poop, which causes pain or constipation.
- They persistently request diapers and become agitated when they do not receive them.

In these cases, it is usually best to pause active training for a few weeks (for example, 2-4 weeks) to relieve the pressure and allow your child to regain control.

"Pausing does not stop you from making progress. In reality, giving your child the space they need to re-engage on their terms helps maintain trust and often accelerates long-term success." — Pediatric Urologist Dr. Marcus Lin.

You can use the following proactive techniques to help you navigate regressions in the future.

- Keep access to your potty charts and stories all year long, even after training has ended.
- Review the potty procedure in a lighthearted and stress-free manner, and regularly use pretend play.
- Always connect the potty to empowerment and choice rather than coercion or demands.

While gently guiding them back to the journey, create an emotionally safe environment where they can say "no" without worrying about punishment.

Tools

Regression Tracker Template

Use this to keep an eye on situations and your responses and identify trends or triggers:

Day	Mishaps	Refused Potty	Emotional State	Trigger/Event
Mon	2	Yes	Tired	Started daycare
Tue	1	No	Calm	Nap skipped

Travel Potty Checklist

Keep this handy for trips:

- Portable potty seat
- Wipes
- Extra underwear & pants
- Snack & hydration
- Potty storybook

- Travel reward chart
- "Potty Hero" badge or stickers

Wrap Up

The regression is a natural and frequently inevitable aspect of developmental progress. It is a gateway to getting to know your child better, understanding their needs, and adjusting your strategy, rather than a failure.

Your child's primary need is for you to stay composed, organized, and patient—whether they are exhausted, distracted, overwhelmed, or just going through a growth spurt. Their best mentor is your steady, compassionate presence.

Our final section will cover long-term success, where we will explore personalized tools and printables to help you stay motivated, including games, charts, trackers, and even reward coupons to provide ongoing inspiration.

10

Personality Perspective

Beyond Your Own

This timeless parenting advice is probably something you have heard countless times, and nowhere is it more evident than during the complex potty training process.

Some children eagerly embrace the challenge of potty training, viewing it as a thrilling new journey. Some may boldly fold their arms, hide behind the couch, or get so absorbed in play that they lose focus mid-pee.

The reason for this wide range of reactions is that potty training is much more than a single developmental milestone; rather, it is a reflection of your child's innate temperament and personality.

"Your child's distinct temperament has a significant impact on how they handle ideas like control, handle changes,

and express their developing independence. Adapting your potty training strategy to fit their unique personality makes the process feel more like a sincere bond than a series of corrections." Child psychologist Dr. Elise Brantley

Four typical toddler temperaments are observed, covering a wide range of toddler personalities. Each has unique needs and approaches success in different ways. They are:

- *The shy observer*
- *The strong-willed boss*
- *The distracted wanderer, and*
- *The anxious overthinker*

Understanding these personalities will enable you to tailor your methods, resulting in a more cohesive and successful potty training experience.

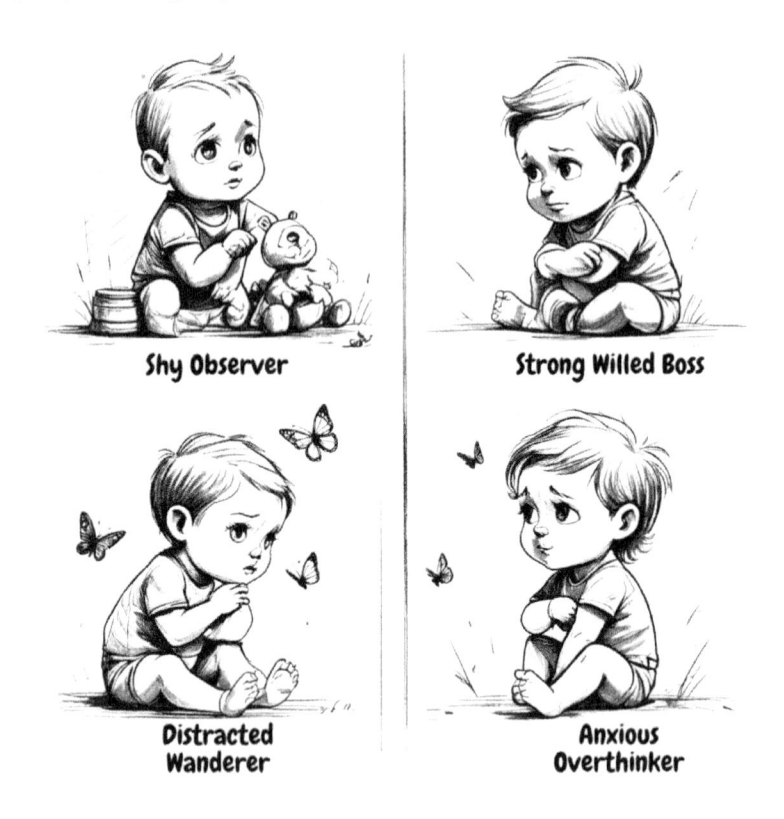

Shy Observer

Strong Willed Boss

Distracted Wanderer

Anxious Overthinker

A Personality Perspective

The Shy Observer

Such toddlers:

- Adjust slowly to new routines or situations.

- Frequently avoids prolonged verbal conversations or direct eye contact, particularly when discussing private issues.
- Easily overwhelmed by perceived pressure, loud praise, or undue attention.
- Prefer a calm environment.

Such traits may lead to their:

- Objection to using the restroom without providing a convincing reason.
- Refusal when their progress is being watched or commented on by many people.
- Failure to communicate their needs often leads to mishaps.

In such situations:

- **Establish a personal restroom for them t**o create a sense of security and personal space. Set up a small, comfortable tent, hang a decorative curtain, or ensure the bathroom has soft, dim lighting.
- **Use storybooks or visual aids for** less verbal prompting or questioning. You can use potty-themed storybooks, charts, and pictures.
- **Provide reinforcement and let** them express themselves by coloring in progress charts, making sticker journals, or drawing scenes from the

bathroom. This enables nonverbal communication and encourages a sense of accomplishment.
- **Use composed language.** For example: "I just noticed that your body became very still. Do you want a trip to the toilet?"
- Such behavior may occasionally indicate that a bathroom check-in is necessary.

The Whispering Potty: A Story

Throughout her potty training journey, Ella, a quiet and reserved girl, didn't say much. Her perceptive parents made a point of letting her sketch how her body felt before she had to go to the bathroom. "My picture wants to go now," Ella whispered after a few silent, unhurried attempts. She had a breakthrough toward independent potty use with this subtle, self-directed communication.

"One piece of advice is that shy children primarily build confidence and comfort through quiet control and subtle acknowledgments, not through loud, effusive praise that might overwhelm them"—behavioral therapist Dr. Marie Hollins.

Strong-Willed Boss

Such toddlers:

- Possess a strong desire for control and a tendency to challenge perceived authority.

- Say "no," even when they may be secretly inclined to cooperate.
- Feel self-sufficient and in control of their choices and actions.

With such traits, they:

- Struggle to maintain control, particularly when using the restroom.
- Intentionally cause mishaps to regain authority or assert their will.
- Are more prone to throwing tantrums if pressure or changes to their routines occur without their consent.

In such situations:

- Provide choices to make them feel in control. For example, you can ask, "Should we tiptoe or run to the potty like superheroes today?" or, "Do you want to use the blue or red potty seat today?"
- Present the achievement charts to capitalize on their competitive and mastery-driven nature. Use systems with levels, badges, or prestigious titles like "Toilet Champion" or "Potty Pro."
- Apply role reversal by asking, "Can you teach your teddy how to go potty all by himself today?" This question encourages children to teach their favorite action figure or teddy bear how to use the restroom.

Leo the Lion: A Story

As a child, Leo was fiercely independent and detested being told what to do. His whole attitude changed, though, when his astute mother appointed him the official "Potty Captain" and gave him a special checklist and a bell to ring for each successful attempt. He jumped right into his new leadership position. On Day 3, he triumphantly roared, "The captain is dry!" as he proudly rang the bell.

"Collaboration and influence work best for strong-willed kids, not strict instructions or orders from superiors. Instead of being a commander, learn to lead from the side as a guide."
— Parent coach Dr. Kenny Maher.

Distracted Wanderers

Such toddlers:

- Often forgets routines or body signals during play.
- Refuses structured potty breaks because that disrupts their flow of activity;
- Are extremely curious, playful, and nearly always on the go. They get easily absorbed in their immediate surroundings.

With such traits

- They frequently delay their bowel movement or urination until the last minute, which causes hurried trips or mishaps.
- They may have more pee mishaps than poop mishaps, as urine urges start earlier.
- They may ignore or miss body cues during intense play,

In such situations,

- **Employ dependable timer cues.** As part of their play, incorporate entertaining, musical alarms or song transitions that indicate a potty break is about to occur.
- **Make bathroom time a performance.** Present it as a brief but intriguing event. "Get Ready for 'The Adventure of Super Flush!' Come on!"
- **Create visual cue cards** that feature pictures or emojis representing standard body signals like "wiggle," "freeze," or "squirm,".
- Make potty routine "a part of the fun by organizing a "race" to the sink", "potty dance," or "a hop to the restroom".

The Treasure Potty: A Story

Maya was an energetic child who would frequently run straight past the restroom while exploring or chasing butterflies. Using star stickers and tiny hints concealed inside the bathroom, her creative father made an intriguing "potty treasure map." Potty time turned into an exciting adventure that she eagerly pursued after she discovered her "gold coin" in the reward box after using the restroom.

"A lot of the time, what seems like a playful diversion is actually how some kids' brains handle changes and new information, not avoidance. The secret is to pique their interest." — Dr. Tara Nunez, an early childhood educator.

The Anxious Overthinker

Such toddlers

- Exhibit extreme caution and consideration for guidelines and standards.
- Look for confirmation that they are doing things correctly.
- Exhibit fear-based withholding due to anxiety about the procedure or its outcome, particularly when it involves bowel movements or poop.

Such traits may lead to

- Constant "what if" queries concerning possible outcomes. For example, "What if the flush is too loud?"
- Excessive worries about mishaps.
- Cry, panic, or freeze when routines change or they feel overburdened.

In such a situations

- **Establish routines with unambiguous visual instructions.** Utilize social stories or step-by-step charts that explain the toilet process.
- Reframe stressful situations: "This is not a perfect day. It is a learning day for your body. Every effort is beneficial."
- Express it in engaging language. "Your body extracts all the energy from your food and then expels it. That is what poop is. Say Good Bye Poops!"

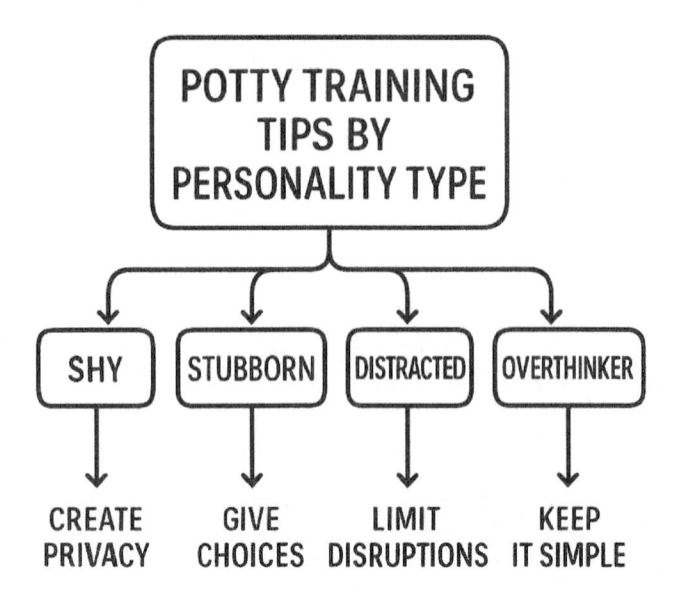

```
                POTTY TRAINING
                   TIPS BY
                PERSONALITY TYPE
                        │
      ┌─────────┬───────┴───────┬──────────┐
      ▼         ▼               ▼          ▼
    SHY     STUBBORN        DISTRACTED  OVERTHINKER
      │         │               │          │
      ▼         ▼               ▼          ▼
   CREATE     GIVE            LIMIT       KEEP
   PRIVACY   CHOICES       DISRUPTIONS  IT SIMPLE
```

The Talking Toilet: A Story

Oliver was always afraid that the toilet would flush with loud, ominous noises. He practiced using the potty with his macho bear, making soft flushing noises. His mother called it "Mr. Flush." to demonstrate how things can be safely disposed of. "Mr. Flush" became his closest companion and confidant.

"More than urgency or speed, anxious toddlers desperately need certainty, predictability, and a great deal of

kindness. Put their emotional well-being first." — Child anxiety specialist Dr. Nina Patel.

Summary

Personality Type	Core Need	Strategy Example	Reinforcement Tool
Shy Observer	Safety & space	Private potty zone, art journal	Gentle stickers, quiet praise
Strong-Willed Boss	Autonomy	Micro-choices, leadership roles	Achievement charts, captain roleplay
Distracted Wanderer	Engagement	Predictable timer cues, movement games	Potty treasure map, visual cues
Anxious Overthinker	Reassurance & certainty	Visual routines, logical stories	Calm scripts, soft toy partner

Your Child, Your Guide

Fit the strategy to your child, not the other way around. Your child is just being themselves; they are not being difficult. You are not only teaching them to use the restroom but also observing their distinct personality and strategically leveraging their innate strengths. Reaffirm their unique identity, create a strong bond of trust, and help them build confidence for all the challenges ahead.

Potty progress is the start of a child's larger developmental journey.

V

Part V: Reinforcement

Real-life success

11

Your Mindset Matters

It Is a Mind Game

Potty training is a profound test of your patience, sense of humor, and innate resilience as a parent before it ever becomes a tangible skill for your toddler.

A moment ago, you were excited about your new pair of trousers. In the next minute, your mischievous toddler might leave some stubborn urine stains on those trousers while looking up at you with his innocent, giggling smile. In those precise, frequently chaotic moments, your response to the mishap, rather than the mishap itself, is what counts.

"Children naturally use our emotions as a model to calibrate and regulate their own." They will panic if we, as parents, panic. They will follow suit and breathe with us if we *can breathe deeply and peacefully."* — Pediatric psychologist Dr. Natalie Klein.

Now let's turn our attention to your mindset. In this whole, frequently tumultuous process, you are the main anchor.

Calm Is Contagious

Children always sense our energy, even if they do not always understand the subtle meaning of what we say. Your steady, calm voice and composed body language provide powerful, unspoken lessons for your child during the messy, chaotic, or frustrating moments of potty training, which are inevitable. Your body language and demeanor inadvertently instruct your child. When you feel frustrated, try repeating these soothing mantras silently:

- "Being in the process of learning is acceptable."
- "Making mistakes is acceptable."
- "Even if the previous attempt didn't go as planned, it is acceptable to try again."
- "This is a temporary phase, not a permanent state."
- "It won't go on forever."
- "I am not performing; I am teaching."
- "My failure curve is different from their learning curve. I'm not failing."

"You are actively and effectively fostering your child's resilience and inherent self-confidence every time you say,

'Oops, that's okay, let's try again.'" — Parent Coach Serena Marks

You can write your favorite mantra on a sticky note. To provide a continuous visual reminder during trying times, place it strategically next to the toilet, on the bathroom mirror, or even on the changing station.

Tag-Team

Potty training is not a solitary activity. Make a conscious effort to divide the workload with your spouse, a helpful friend, an understanding grandparent, or even a reliable babysitter. When the entire experience isn't dependent on one person's patience or energy, your child gains a lot. A successful tag team follows:

- **Different shifts:** A tag team approach should enable mental breaks and split the day so that one parent handles the mornings while the other handles the afternoons.
- **Trade positions:** One parent can take care of cleaning up after a mishap while the other diverts the child's attention from the "mess" by telling them a reassuring story or providing a fun diversion.
- **Process signals from your partners:** Establish a quick phrase or nonverbal cue to let the other parent

know when one parent is feeling overburdened and needs to take over right away.

Jessica, a mother of two, revealed, "My husband and I had an obvious rule: If one of us felt our voice starting to rise, the other would instantly step in with humor or a silly distraction." "It turned into a delightful and successful method of controlling ourselves and averting tantrums."

Celebration Time

Every journey includes small wins, too. There will be plenty of moments when you feel inspired to celebrate your potty training journey. Don't hesitate to acknowledge and celebrate these small wins.

- Did your child go three days in a row without assistance to urinate?
- Did your child use the potty at least once a day without any help?
- Did they explicitly tell you that they left after a mishap?
- Did they not resist sitting on the potty for a couple of seconds?

"The fundamental components of confidence are micro-successes. Youngsters are extremely sensitive; they get a far more profound sense of progress from your positive tone and

steady manner than they do from simple chart tally marks."
— Child Development Specialist Dr. Karen Lee

Celebrate uniquely! Create absurd "potty songs." In front of the mirror, give enthusiastic high-fives. Share an energetic update with Grandma over the phone.

Your child absorbs the vital lesson, "Trying is good." Each time you genuinely celebrate even the smallest progress, your child gets the message that their efforts are being recognized and valued.

The Silence

It's not easy to raise kids. Potty training is just one of those challenging moments. There will be instances when you feel completely drained and want to cry out loud. Don't lose your heart. You are making all the right strides to make your toddler independent. The following indicators show that you need to take a break.

- You find yourself dreading every prompt or interaction about the toilet.
- Your child is demonstrating resistance in almost every situation, not just when using the restroom.
- You both seem to be crying more than you are trying to use the restroom.

- You frequently experience intense frustration, rage, or a sense of defeat.
- Don't worry. Every parent goes through this inflection point. Remember this:
- Calling a timeout when you are feeling overwhelmed is perfectly acceptable.
- Feel free to take a break if your child is crying uncontrollably. There could be other reasons.
- You can replenish your emotional reserves and, most importantly, restore a sense of joy and lightheartedness to the process with even a brief break (24–72 hours).

"Slowing down does not mean giving up. Maintaining your relationship and your child's growing sense of trust is a profound gift that you give to both of you." — Parenting counselor Dr. Linny Zhao

The Hidden Potty Seat: A Story

After two seemingly "mishap-free" and successful days, Caroline, a sweet 2.5-year-old with a growing penchant for mischief, abruptly and mysteriously refused to participate in potty training. On a particularly memorable morning, her mother found the potty seat ingeniously concealed in the laundry hamper.

Her astute parents cleverly made it into a game rather than using force or frustration. The "potty detective," Caroline, was tasked with figuring out where the silly potty seat would hide every morning. In just two days, she was back to her regular toilet routine, laughing, and completely involved.

Playful interaction and humor can create opportunities to revitalize your environment and get everything back on track with potty training.

Forgiveness Toolkit

Inevitably, you will occasionally become angry. Or make a last-ditch bribe. Sometimes, you might decide against taking a bath due to your inability to handle another situation involving moisture or cleaning. Forgive yourself when these moments unavoidably arise.

You might include a few chores in your forgiveness toolkit:

- Write a private journal entry where you express your worst day and all the frustrations you are experiencing.
- Listen to a reassuring voicemail from a reliable friend who says, "You are doing great; you have got this."
- Listen to the music you've always loved.

- Establish a specific routine for resetting your bedtime, even if it simply involves spending a few more minutes quietly cuddling with your child.

Remember this: You are actively teaching someone how to use a toilet. That is an incredible achievement, my friend.

"With little sleep, a never-ending pile of laundry, and the overwhelming pressure to do everything flawlessly for our kids, we are all doing our best." — Eliza Jordan, mother and pediatric nurse

Restart

It's a long and challenging journey that requires many breaks to regain your energy. Take a moment to reflect on whether we are heading in the right direction. Occasionally, you may need to consciously decide to start over after a necessary pause or even a significant setback.

Some of you might think it's bad news. No, it's not because you're not starting from scratch. You and your child are beginning from a position of valuable experience with some understanding of each other.

> **PROGRESS OVER PERFECTION**
> **LAUGH, THEN, FLUSH**
> **YOU'RE GREAT**

Reset Phrase

Restart With Self-Assurance

Restarting is a great way to ensure you are motivated to help your toddler become independent. It can be exhausting but also reassuring. However, before you restart:

- Have clear communication with your child. "We're going to help your incredible body remember how to

use the potty again after we took a brief break. Together, we will accomplish it."
- Permit your toddler to select an intriguing new toilet-related item. A brand-new, blank sticker chart, a special pack of underwear, or a new potty seat can all spark new excitement.
- Employ a seasonal metaphor or a new character from the story. A "Sunshine Potty Pal" for summer or a "Potty Penguin" for winter can help them use their imagination again.
- Put more emphasis on having fun and the journey rather than just the end goal. Instead of concentrating on the pressure of instant dryness, enjoy the process of learning and trying.

"When we had to start over, we called it our potty comeback tour. We even composed an absurd theme song for it. It completely altered the atmosphere." Dylan, an Oregon father, said.

Be the Calm You Want to See

Fundamentally, potty training is more than just getting your pants dry. It is a profoundly transformative journey. It requires a great deal of patience and compels you to give up on the unattainable goal of perfection. Leaning deeply into love is necessary, particularly when things become unquestionably soggy. It involves assimilating the critical realization that your serene demeanor is your most effective training aid.

    So when you feel stressed, take a deep breath, engage in a silly dance, and enjoy a hearty laugh at the mishaps that are sure to happen. This way, you significantly influence your child's resilience, trust, and positive self-image while also helping them develop a valuable skill.

12

Real Success

The toilet itself is never the only aspect of potty training. A tribute to birth parents putting forth their best efforts on actual carpeted floors, this journey is interlaced with humor, hope, and resilience. The real success of potty training can only be measured by the smiles on parents' faces as they witness their toddlers' incredible journey of independence. Here are real-life stories from a diverse range of parents, guardians, grandparents, and dedicated caregivers who have overcome the inevitable challenges of achieving toddlers' independence from diapers. You will encounter numerous challenges across various ages, seasons, personalities, and potty training methods. Still, one crucial factor that will keep you on track to achieve your goal is your toddler's progress. These stories serve as a powerful reminder that you are not alone and that, like thousands of other parents, this approach will work with a bit of patience and a smile.

A Silent Girl: A Springtime Tale

Name: 2.5-year-old Sophie Characteristic: Shy Observer Time of year: Spring

The Issue: Sophie had a severe dislike of noise. She always refused to sit on the potty and would reflexively cover her ears whenever the toilet flushed. Despite their very gentle approach, nothing had inspired her.

What Worked: Then one day, her astute mother created a "butterfly potty garden" by carefully applying vibrant flower stickers to the bathroom wall that made the area look welcoming. After that, whenever her parents gently reminded Sophie to sit on the potty, she would bring her favorite toy butterfly to "visit the garden."

Breakthrough: Something interesting happened on Day 3. "She wants to try now," Sophie whispered to her mother while pointing to a sticker of flowers on the wall. First, her butterfly tried the beautiful potty garden, and then, without further encouragement, Sophie did the same with assurance.

We realized that we needed to stop pushing and start playing for real. That one change in our strategy completely transformed Sophie's life.

The Flushing Boy: A Winter Tale

Name: Jackson, age three. Personality: Overthinking and anxious, Winter

The Issue: Jackson had an exceptionally vivid imagination, which unfortunately led to the assumption that the toilet was "too loud and too deep." He experienced severe discomfort as a result of holding his urine for hours because of this fear.

What Worked: His encouraging father imaginatively read him "Santa's Potty Pass," a fanciful, made-up tale about how Santa's reindeer had to learn how to use the restroom quietly before they could take off on their enchanted flight on Christmas Eve. By creating a "magic flush button" out of a basic cardboard switch that produced a soothing, quiet sound when pushed, they allayed his concerns.

Breakthrough: On Christmas Eve, Jackson proudly flushed his feces and exclaimed, "Now I am ready for Santa!" Excitement took the place of fear.

"A potent technique for helping kids externalize and eventually control their fears related to the toileting process is story-based desensitization." — Child Behavior Specialist Dr. Simone Beck.

A Strong Girl: A Fall Tale

Name: Riley, age two, Strong-willed personality, Leader, Time of year: fall

The Issue: Riley automatically said "NO!" to essentially all the potty tricks. Potty time soon turned into a never-ending power struggle between her and her progressively worn-out mother.

What Worked: Her creative grandmother cleverly turned potty training into an exciting game show. Riley was awarded "Potty Star of the Week" and given a makeshift microphone to announce every bathroom break.

Breakthrough: Encouraged by the attention, Riley started asking her teddy bear to attend her "performances" on Day 2. "It felt like she needed the spotlight and to be in charge—and once we gave it to her, she ran with it," her mother said.

A Distracted Boy: A Summer Tale

Adam, a 22-month-old distracted explorer with a Distracted Wanderer personality, type: Summer.

The Issue: Adam was a naturally distracted wanderer; he loved to run around and explore different things, dig in the garden, or observe fascinating insects in his small box. Adam often faced mishaps outside because he was too absorbed in his activities to pay attention to his body's signals.

What Worked: His ingenious father built a distinctive "pee tent" in the backyard, transforming it into a welcoming area with vibrant jungle animal stickers and a colorful mat. Each time Adam used the restroom inside the tent, he received a leaf to add to the growing "jungle wall," which served as a visual record of his development.

Breakthrough: A clear sign of self-direction emerged on Day 3. Without any further prompting, Adam sat on the toilet, wholly absorbed in his "jungle adventure," after asking proactively, "Can my frog go too?"

Thought: "He needed a specific location that felt entirely different from just another area of our house and more like his own outdoor space."

The Twins: A Story

Names: three-year-old Emma and Ethan. Personalities: Ethan = Strong-Willed, Emma = Anxious Overthinker Leader Season: Year-round

The issue was that Emma felt anxious and often asked "what if" questions about the potty process, while Ethan turned everything into a power struggle and demanded control.

What Worked: To appeal to each twin's personality, the parents developed a creative, color-coded schedule. For example, Ethan's "action hero" persona was represented by red, while Emma's "peaceful penguin" approach was symbolized by blue.

Emma received the assurance she desperately needed through a comprehensive checklist featuring comforting images. Ethan was given superhero tokens as a reward for his achievements, fueling his ambition.

Breakthrough: On Day 3, they naturally began reminding each other to wash their hands and flush, which was a truly remarkable moment. "They became each other's coaches, encouraging each other, their mother said. It was truly a sight to behold.

"Even though their styles are very different, siblings frequently possess a unique ability to support and encourage one another during important developmental milestones," said family psychologist Dr. Corey Jenkins.

The Flight: A Story

Liam is two years and ten months old. Area of Concern: Flying to Grandma's House.

Problem: Liam's parents were concerned that the upcoming flight would undo their hard work and disrupt their routine.

What Worked: They brought a personalized photo book called "Liam and the Flying Flush," a foldable potty seat, and a laminated sticker chart for consistency. Like a professional pilot doing a pre-flight inspection, Liam was urged to "check" the airplane potty before takeoff to make it an adventure.

Breakthrough: In the middle of the flight, Liam proudly and with the assurance of a true leader declared, "I have to pee like a captain!" and marched down the aisle to the airplane restroom, much to the relief and pride of his parents.

Lesson: Using proper planning resources, captivating tales, and an optimistic outlook can prevent travel from impeding potty training progress. Instead, it can become another opportunity for achievement.

The Fridge Manifesto

A manifesto is required to keep you motivated. You can think of it as your daily reset button. Keep it close at hand as a continual source of motivation, tape it next to the toilet, or place it prominently on your refrigerator.

Manifesto of Potty Parents

The Manifesto of the Potty Parent

- Even when the floor beneath me is wet, I remain composed.
- Even if the underwear is still wet, I have patience.
- I recall that every mishap is an essential component of progress.

- When I inevitably lose my composure, I forgive myself.
- Every little "yes," every little step forward, will be celebrated by me.
- My child will follow this journey, and I will keep pace with it.
- This is not a competition between kids.
- This is not a test of my parenting style's success or failure; I will always cherish this priceless moment.
- My child chirped, "Daddy, I can do it." I whispered back, "I know you can."

Concluding Remarks

This potty training is far from over, even when the last diaper leaves your house. It ends when your child is taller, not just because they made it to the bathroom, but because, with your help, they overcame a major developmental obstacle. That is your most significant and enduring victory of all.

13

APPENDIX: Tools, Charts & Resources

This appendix is designed to provide you with practical, ready-to-use support through essential checklists, engaging charts, and heartwarming downloadable stories. These resources are crafted to make your potty training journey smoother and more successful.

Age-Specific Readiness Checklists (18 months–4 years)

Every child develops at their own unique pace, but this quick-reference readiness guide can help you assess their current stage. Utilize this checklist during your initial 3-day observation phase to gauge their preparedness.

18–24 Months: The Curious Explorer

May Be Ready If They:

- **Mimic toileting behavior:** They follow you into the bathroom, curious about what you are doing, or pretend to use the potty with their dolls.
- **Stay dry for at least 1–2 hours:** This indicates their bladder is developing the capacity to hold urine for more extended periods.
- **Show discomfort in dirty or wet diapers:** They might pull at their diaper, fuss, or ask for a change.
- **Use basic signs or words:** They communicate simple needs using words like "poo," "pee," "wet," or "done," or through distinct gestures.
- **Can sit still for 2–3 minutes:** This is crucial for successful potty attempts.

Not Quite Ready If:

- **Hide to poop but resist the potty:** They seek privacy for bowel movements but refuse to use the toilet.
- **Get upset when their diaper is removed:** They show distress or anxiety about being without a diaper.

- **Do not respond to prompts or changes:** *They seem unaware or indifferent to efforts to engage them in potty training.*

24–36 Months: The Power Seeker

May Be Ready If They:

- **Communicate clearly about needs:** *They can articulate when they need to go or have gone, often with more complex sentences.*
- **Show strong interest in "big kid" routines:** *They express a desire to do things like older siblings or peers, including using the toilet.*
- **Can pull pants up/down independently:** *This demonstrates the fine motor skills necessary for self-sufficiency.*
- **Understand basic reward systems:** *They respond positively to praise, stickers, or small incentives.*

Not Quite Ready If:

- **Enter tantrum cycles at the mere idea of the potty:** *Strong emotional resistance indicates they are feeling pressured.*
- **Fear of bathroom-related tools or flushing: Anxiety around the toilet, the flush sound, or the** *potty seat may be present.*

- *Still rely on diapers for comfort or security:* They view diapers as a safe, comforting constant.

36–48 Months: The Rule Learner

May Be Ready If They:

- *Show pride in independence and self-care:* They enjoy demonstrating new skills and taking care of themselves.
- *Ask to wear underwear consistently:* This signifies a strong internal motivation to move past diapers.
- *Want to be like peers/siblings:* Social motivation plays a larger role at this age.
- *Respond well to charts and verbal praise:* They thrive on positive reinforcement and visual tracking of progress.

Not Quite Ready If:

- *Use the potty as a control or protest tool:* They intentionally resist or have mishaps to assert their will.
- *Refuse even with positive incentives:* Their resistance outweighs any external motivation.

Get anxious around performance expectations: They feel undue pressure to be "perfect" and fear failure.

Seasonal Story Summaries (with Morals)

These short, engaging stories are designed to help toddlers relate to the potty training process through imaginative narratives, making it more accessible and fun.

Spring – "Buzz the Bee's Big Day"

Summary: *Buzz the Bee feels a flutter in his belly, but he's scared of the big flower potty in his hive because of its echoing sounds. With gentle encouragement and the soft tinkling of nearby wind chimes, Buzz and his brave pet caterpillar discover that trying something new can be surprisingly harmonious.*

Moral: Trying something new is brave—even if you buzz a little first.

Summer – "The Garden Fairy's Golden Seat"

Summary: *A radiant garden fairy, with her shimmering wings, takes on the delightful task of teaching her playful squirrel friends how to use the special "leaf mats" and "golden petals" for going potty outdoors, keeping their magical garden pristine.*

Moral: Going potty helps keep the garden clean—and makes you feel incredibly proud.

Autumn – "Leafy Larry's Big Leap"

Summary: *Leafy Larry, a hesitant little leaf, is initially afraid of making the big leap from his tree, just as he's apprehensive about sitting on the potty. But once he takes that brave plunge, he discovers a soft, safe, and surprisingly comfortable landing.*

Moral: Sometimes change feels scary, but it very often leads to something much better.

Winter – "Snow Bunny's Warm Surprise"

Summary: *Snow Bunny, accustomed to the cozy comfort of his blanket burrow, does not want to leave his warm spot. However, he learns that the potty is even more comfortable when his feet stay wonderfully dry, and he discovers a delightful warmth that awaits him.*

Moral: It is okay to leave your comfort zone when love and warmth are waiting for you.

Holiday – "Santa's Potty Pass"

Summary: *Santa Claus begins handing out special "Potty Passes" to his reindeer, who must learn to go potty by themselves before their big Christmas Eve flight. One little* *reindeer is terrified of the process until he receives cheerful encouragement and learns to celebrate each small step.*

Moral: Everyone learns at their own pace. Celebrating each step, no matter how small, is truly magical.

Reward Charts

These visual reinforcement tools are perfect for tracking progress, celebrating effort, and motivating your child throughout their potty training journey.

Superhero Chart (For Boys & Girls)

- **Each time your child successfully uses the potty, they earn a special "power badge" sticker** *to place on their chart.*
- **After collecting five badges,** *they earn a "Super Cape" (a designated towel or blanket to wear proudly).*
- **After collecting 10 badges,** *they get a "Super Snack of Choice" (a small, desired treat).*
- **Download at:** *www.coralcubs.com/resources/potty-training*

Fairy Chart (Girls)

- *Color a fairy wing each day she stays dry* for the entire day.
- *3 wings colored* = She earns a magical "fairy dust glitter jar" (a small jar of glitter).
- *7 wings colored* = She gets a new, enchanting fairy story time before bed.
- **Download at:** *www.coralcubs.com/resources/potty-training*

Animal Adventure (All Toddlers)

- *Mark their progress with cheerful paw prints* on a winding path.
- *Reach the forest potty cave after five stops* on the path, symbolizing a mini-milestone.
- *Arrive at the finish line* = They earn an honorary "Potty Explorer" medal (a homemade paper medal or a small toy medal).

Download at: *www.coralcubs.com/resources/potty-training*

Nighttime Tracker Chart (7-Night Dry Streak)

Use this simple chart to gently track your child's nighttime dryness progress over a week, using encouraging symbols.

Night	Dry? ☑ or ✗	Sticker Earned	Special Note
1			
2			
3			
4			
5			
6			
7			🎉 You Did It! 🎉

Tips for Nighttime Tracking:

- ***Reward effort, not just perfection:*** *Praise attempts to get up or communicate, even if an mishap occurred.*
- ***Celebrate at 3-night and 7-night streaks:*** *These smaller milestones build momentum and confidence.*
- ***Use a special "Goodnight Potty Friend" plush:*** *Let them choose a plush toy to sleep with, symbolizing comfort and encouragement.*

Download complete template:
www.coralcubs.com/resources/potty-training

Link to Downloadable Printables & Audio Stories

To access all of these valuable printable tools, engaging charts, and bonus audio versions of the seasonal stories, follow the link below:

Visit: *www.coralcubs.com/resources/potty-training*

This comprehensive resource page includes:

- **High-resolution printable reward charts** for various personalities and motivations.
- **You can personalize the editable readiness checklists to suit your child's** specific developmental stage.
- **"Buzz the Bee" and "Santa's Potty Pass" available as MP3 bedtime audio files**, perfect for winding down.
- **The nighttime tracker, complete with editable fields, allows** for flexible progress monitoring.

You can easily structure your potty training days with the help of daily ritual planner templates.